W9-BTR-332

Perfecting Your
GOLF SWING

Perfecting Your GOLF SWING

New Ways to Lower Your Score

Oliver Heuler

Sterling Publishing Co., Inc.   New York

Contents

Preface

I met Oliver Heuler five years ago at one of the golf seminars I gave in Hamburg, Germany. He immediately caught my attention because of his incredible thirst for knowledge. He literally showered me with precise and detailed questions, primarily about the techniques of the game. At that time, Oliver already had an excellent golf swing, acquired by studying the literature and by checking out and practising all kinds of theories and methods. Of course, such an analytical approach did not further his career as a player, but a golf teacher must be knowledgeable and be able to convey this knowledge to his students in simple and effective ways.

Right from the beginning, Oliver made use of the video camera, with the result that his students progressed much faster than others taught traditionally. This book is an astounding achievement for such a young teacher. Using excellent photos and drawings, he successfully conveys to the reader the latest findings about the swing, putting, approach shots, and the bunker game.

I wish you lots of fun, and hope that reading this book will make you a better player, on the driving range as well as on the golf course.

Yours,

Denis Pugh

Teaching Director of the David Leadbetter Academy of Golf, Quiet Water, Essex, England

Introduction

Why Is Golf So Hard?

For most of us, golf is a difficult game. Is it possible that we all just lack talent or intelligence? I don't believe so. I think the problem lies with the difficulty of the assignment: using a long-handled club to hit a small ball with force and precision again and again. The ball has to be hit not only for distance but with accuracy. For instance, when using a wood the face of the club cannot be angled more than 1 degree off for the ball to reach the fairway. In addition, in golf a player not only does not have three tries to accomplish the called-upon feat (as is the case in some other sports), but it has to happen over 70 times in one round.

Of course, other sports, such as the high jump, surfing, and ski jumping, are also technically very difficult. But generally speaking, only athletically talented, young people play these sports. Golf is different. Almost everyone can play golf. Mistakes rarely result in injuries—one of the major reasons why those blessed with less than perfect motor skills or athletic abilities enthusiastically embrace the sport. And golf is so much fun precisely because it is so difficult. Players would get bored if they could master the sport after only a few lessons. Many, however, make the mistake of comparing themselves to players who are good athletes, and that has to be discouraging. Another cause for frustration is that in playing golf we are not simply using natural movements, such

Although true perfection can never be achieved, Nick Faldo's golf swing comes about as close to it as possible, producing consistently long drives.

as walking or running, and cannot afford to rely on our instincts. On the contrary, our instinctive reactions are usually wrong. For instance, if a ball curves to the right, we automatically try to direct our swing to the left. But as we quickly discover, that does not solve the problem—it only makes it worse.

In golf, one mistake leads to another. Ignored, a bad swing consists of an endless succession of mistakes and attempts to correct them. The player never achieves the desired consistency. To avoid such a dilemma, the beginner should try to learn the proper golf swing, and the advanced player should try to eliminate any faulty sequence of movements.

New Ways of Playing Golf

The search for the perfect swing is as old as golf itself. The means of achieving it, however, have become much easier in the last couple of years because:
- Sports scientists, who used to consider golf as the most boring kind of social entertainment, pursued only by millionaires, now include golf in their research.
- Video cameras permit the analysis of mistakes that cannot be seen with the naked eye.
- Golf instructors today have far more knowledge. They often receive rigorous training and participate in a worldwide exchange of ideas.

If you want to improve your golf swing, look to Nick Faldo from England. He is the best. In spite of considerable success and winning many tournaments in Europe, in 1985 he decided to totally change his swing . . .

. . . because he knew that he could only reach his goal of becoming the number-one player in the world by acquiring a neutral swing that would result in consistent shots. . . .

most in your mind: There is no such thing as perfection in golf. Even the most successful professional players will tell you that only 15 percent of their shots are perfect. That is a long way from an ideal round of 32 shots on a par 72 course. To date, the best round ever played in a tournament was 59.

Let me briefly return to the secret of successful golf. If such a secret exists at all, with regard to executing a full swing, it might go like this: As the player executes

The results of these changes have contributed greatly to an understanding of the very complex sequence of movements involved in swinging a club. New insights have drastically changed many accepted theories.

In the past, golf instructors often wanted to simplify the game. They established general rules that, as we know today, actually made the game more difficult.

When I teach, my students always want me to give them one decisive tip that will permit them to play *the* perfect game. Of course, you cannot learn a good golf swing in one week or from one tip. The time it takes to learn a correct swing depends to a large degree on the individual and the intensity and quality of practice.

One thing, however, should be fore-

the swing, the face of the club, pointed squarely in the direction of the goal, must consistently hit the ball at high speed, and always on the sweet spot.

Of course, this is nothing new. But the way to achieve this goal is different today.

One thing is certain: You will only be wasting your time if you try to find the "secret" by going to the driving range and hitting ball after ball with grim determination.

There is only one way to succeed: You must find out how the actual impact on the ball differs from the ideal; then you will know what in the sequence of movements is responsible for the result.

The behavior of the ball in the air lets us examine the moment of impact (see page 80). When analyzing a movement, you must distinguish between cause and effect. Obviously it is not very helpful to tell a player that he raises his head at the same time as the club hits the ball. When the club approaches the ball at too steep an angle, it might be good advice to suggest that a player "grow taller" as he hits through the ball, to avoid breaking his wrist hitting a deep divot. But a club is usually too steep because the face of the club is too open. (If you don't want to constantly be looking for your ball in the rough to your right, you will instinctively swing to the left, with the clubface tilted to the right. The club will then be at a steep angle at impact.)

Once you recognize and correct the reasons for flawed techniques, you will experience the real joy of golf.

The Golf Swing: Individually Different?

Of course, golfers play the game many different ways. This becomes clear when you watch professional players during a tournament. They often use very different techniques. However, certain physical movements are ideal. For instance, the club should always remain on a certain

. . . After two years without any success, he won the Spanish and British Open in spectacular fashion. Ever since then, his game has been at the highest level. Already many people consider him to be one of the most successful players in the history of golf.

plane during the swing, and, while rotating around the spine, the body must remain in the same position that the player assumed at the beginning of the shot.

Anatomically we all differ, so a swing might look different for different people. This is why we talk in relative rather than absolute terms. For instance, it would not be very helpful to describe or define the position and distance between a player's feet in terms of inches or centimetres. The relative term used will be "shoulder-width." Although the goal is the same for all of us, the methods might differ from one player to the next.

If, for instance, a player's hands are too far to the right, they must be turned farther to the left to achieve a neutral grip (see page 18). If, on the other hand, another player holds the club too far to the left, the exact opposite must be done to achieve the same goal, a neutral grip.

A third player may seem to break all

the rules and still come up with astounding results. We can be sure that there are other reasons responsible for the quality of a shot. In general, we can list three reasons:

• Talent
• Technique
• Training

A good player is usually above average in two of the three. Those who are counted among the top players in the field are, generally speaking, proficient in all three. If golf is your hobby and you don't have a natural talent for the game, you'll have to work harder to learn the correct techniques than a professional player

would because the professional already has a greater intuitive feeling for ball and body movements that compensates for possible technical shortcomings.

How to Get the Most Out of This Book

A beginner should read this book systematically, from cover to cover. A more advanced player must decide whether or not to start from scratch, examining all aspects of preparing for a shot (grip, posture, stance, address position) as well as the swing itself, making all necessary changes, or simply study ways to improve the flight path of the ball with as few changes as possible. Relearning requires time and patience but usually yields the best and most consistent results. To analyze and change only what seems necessary at the time is very difficult but can often bring very quick improvements. For this to happen, a player must be able to correctly analyze the flight of the ball and (using the chapter on correcting mistakes) be able to determine the reasons for the mistakes. Combining both methods would be a way to acquire a correct technique. However, the sequence of the corrections a player makes depends on the way the ball behaves in flight. In other words, in the beginning, always start with corrections that improve the behavior of the ball in the air.

The chapter on the short game can be worked through independent of the one on the long game and is particularly valuable to the player for whom changing his swing seems too risky. Improvements are relatively risk free, but a good swing does not make a good golfer. The proper strategy for play on any given course is often

Bernhard Langer owes much of his success to hard training. Today, he is considered one of the psychologically strongest and tactically most advanced golf professionals in the world.

as responsible for the score as the technique used for long shots. A more detailed inquiry into this topic, however, is beyond the scope of this book.

If you are left-handed, you must reverse all terms relating to the swing. For you, a club tilted to the right becomes a club tilted to the left. The photos and drawings in this book are for right-handers. If they annoy you, here is a trick that I always use to help left-handers: Hold a mirror up to the book and look at the illustration in the mirror.

Basically, analyzing the swing of a left-hander isn't that much more difficult than analyzing the swing of a right-hander; however, since fewer people are left-handed, it takes a bit more time for the teacher to "see" what he is looking at. In my opinion, too few left-handers play golf. While overall the number of left-handers is about 5 percent of the population, among golf players it is less than 1 percent. In the past, left-handers had difficulty finding clubs. However, golf instructors are not all blameless. A theory, still widely held today, states that a right-hander plays the game primarily with the left side of the body. This means that, when swinging the club, the left arm and the left part of the upper and lower body is dominant. Following this reasoning, a left-hander should play just like a right-hander, because a left-hander's strong side *is* the left side. Therefore, left-handers would "normally" use clubs made for right-handers. (According to this logic, right-handers should be using clubs specifically made for left-handers!) But left-handers, if they swing from the right side, have to carry out complicated movements from their weaker, right side. For example, the right arm flexes during the backswing and downswing, while the left arm remains straight throughout. Also, their right hand, positioned below the left hand on the grip, must stretch farther. Therefore, a left-hander, regardless of the theory discussed above, should use clubs made for left-handers and right-handers should use clubs made for them.

Players who seem to be standing on the "wrong" side should not rush out and sell their clubs because, in my experience, the difference is not as great as you might think. In order to gain a better understanding, I played left-handed for a while. In the beginning, it felt very awkward, but after I practised for a while, I realized that the differences were not all that great, and my game became rather good.

I have one piece of advice for beginners: Whatever you do, play from your "natural" side. For more advanced players: Change only if you are experiencing extreme problems when playing from your "wrong" side.

If you are left-handed and just starting out, by all means use clubs made for left-handers and swing from the left side. Advanced players should only change if they have serious problems.

To successfully play this course built by Gary Player in South Africa's Sun City, you have to play the long ball: the course measures 7691 yards (7033 m) with a par of 76.

Before Taking the SHOT

Grip

Learning to hold your club properly requires patience and practice. Of course, no one would expect a weekend golfer to swing a club the way a professional does, but why not learn the proper grip?

Many players hold a club improperly right from the beginning because they don't understand the importance of the grip. They concentrate on their swing, assuming that most mistakes are made there. But a faulty grip always leads to a faulty swing. A proper grip is essential to a proper swing.

If you are an advanced player and you're feeling awkward with the suggestions outlined here, don't be discouraged. Even an improved grip feels strange in the beginning. Be patient and diligent. In no time, you'll feel as if you have always held your golf clubs this way.

Hold the club handle diagonally across the palm of your left hand.

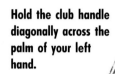

Function of the Grip

The main function of a proper grip is to bring the clubhead to the ball at the right angle. In order to understand how the grip controls the clubface, you must know that, at the moment of impact, the hands tend to fall into a natural position without rotation. (This is due to the great speed built up during the swing.) If, for instance, you are holding the club at address too far to the left or right, and the clubhead is correctly behind the ball, during the swing your hands will return automatically to their natural position, and at the moment of impact the clubface will rotate to the right or left, respectively. The ball will then start out in the wrong direction and veer off even farther because of the side-spin.

A proper grip allows you to flex your wrist towards the thumb (radial flexion), increasing the speed with which the clubface hits the ball. When you bend your upper body slightly forward (as is the custom in golf) and let your arms hang down at your sides, totally relaxed, you will notice that the back of your hands, if you brought the back upper edges together, would form something like a right angle. Very often we hear that the back of the hands should be parallel to each other when gripping a club. From a physiological point of view this is wrong, and such a position interferes when the wrists need to be flexed. Actually, when you hold a club correctly, the backs of your hands form a 30 degree angle.

Since the force created by an improperly hit ball or by a clubhead hitting the ground too hard transfers from the club to your arms, a correct grip absorbs much of the force. If too much of the grip rests in the palm of the hands, the full force of the impact transfers to the elbow, resulting in the so-called golfer's arm. The best way to

The club "falls" into your left hand when the arm hangs in a relaxed fashion alongside your body.

prevent golfer's arm is to give the fingers more responsibility for holding the handle. As you can see, a proper grip is not only responsible for the direction and the length of your drive but also prevents injury.

The Grip in Detail

At the outset, let me say that there is no such thing as the right grip for everybody. And while we're talking about basic concepts, here are two that can be applied to all players. First, rotating the hands when holding a club depends on the direction of the flight of the ball. A chronic slicer should not hold the club the same way as a hooker. Secondly, the position of the little finger of the right hand depends on the size of the player's hand. We'll discuss both of these details more extensively later in this chapter. However, don't change your grip from one shot to the next. The grip is the same in all situations, except when putting or chipping.

Hold the club so that the handle rests diagonally in the palm of your left hand, touching the first digit of your index finger. Allow your arm to hang relaxed next to your body and close your fingers as you let the club "fall" into your hand. The thumb and pad of your hand will automatically be on top. Hold the club between the pad of your hand, the pad of the thumb, and the thumb in such a way that the end of the handle is still visible.

Position the thumb slightly to the right of center at the upper part of the handle. You can find the proper "length" for the thumb by stretching it down as far as possible and memorizing that spot. The ideal position is exactly between that spot and the original position of the thumb. This position ensures that the club does not swing back too far, because the "shorter" the thumb's position on the handle, the more restricted the swing.

A neutral grip is one in which you hold the club directly in front of you. You can easily see the knuckles of the index and middle fingers. A V, formed by the thumb and the upper edge of the back of your hand (an extension of the left index finger), will point to the middle of your right collarbone. If you can see more or less of your knuckles, your hand is too far to the left or right, respectively. In addition, you should not be able to see any part of the handle of the club when looking down at your hand; otherwise the hands are too far to the left or the pad of your little finger is not on, but to the left of, the handle. In that case, the handle is between the pad of the little finger and the pad of the thumb instead of below both. In this position, you'll find it extremely difficult to flex your wrists, and your hand often rotates too far to the left, causing you to slice. This is one of the most common mistakes.

Place your middle and ring fingers of the right hand on the handle from below.

To find the position for your right hand, hold the club in your left hand in front of you. Then from below, put the first digit of the middle and ring fingers at the point of the handle that is on the opposite side of the left thumb. As soon as you close both fingers, the tips of the fingers will touch the left thumb at the left side.

Position the little finger of the right hand between the index and middle fingers of the left hand, creating an overlapping grip. Next, put the palm of the right

When assuming a neutral grip, the knuckles of your index and middle fingers are visible on the left hand (below middle). **The tips of your right index and middle fingers touch the left thumb on its left side** (below right).

One of the most common mistakes: The pad of your left thumb is to the left of the upper part of the handle.

PGA West in California is a classic example of a Pete Dye course. Playing it is a memorable experience for every golfer. Its spectacular layout made Paul (Pete) Dye one of the most famous golf-course architects in the world.

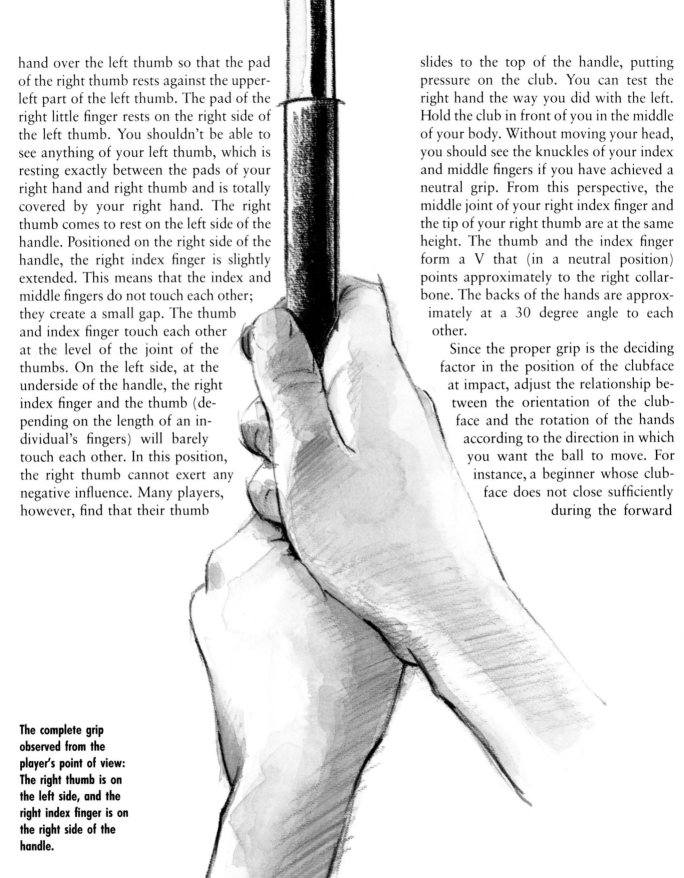

hand over the left thumb so that the pad of the right thumb rests against the upper-left part of the left thumb. The pad of the right little finger rests on the right side of the left thumb. You shouldn't be able to see anything of your left thumb, which is resting exactly between the pads of your right hand and right thumb and is totally covered by your right hand. The right thumb comes to rest on the left side of the handle. Positioned on the right side of the handle, the right index finger is slightly extended. This means that the index and middle fingers do not touch each other; they create a small gap. The thumb and index finger touch each other at the level of the joint of the thumbs. On the left side, at the underside of the handle, the right index finger and the thumb (depending on the length of an individual's fingers) will barely touch each other. In this position, the right thumb cannot exert any negative influence. Many players, however, find that their thumb

slides to the top of the handle, putting pressure on the club. You can test the right hand the way you did with the left. Hold the club in front of you in the middle of your body. Without moving your head, you should see the knuckles of your index and middle fingers if you have achieved a neutral grip. From this perspective, the middle joint of your right index finger and the tip of your right thumb are at the same height. The thumb and the index finger form a V that (in a neutral position) points approximately to the right collarbone. The backs of the hands are approximately at a 30 degree angle to each other.

Since the proper grip is the deciding factor in the position of the clubface at impact, adjust the relationship between the orientation of the clubface and the rotation of the hands according to the direction in which you want the ball to move. For instance, a beginner whose clubface does not close sufficiently during the forward

The complete grip observed from the player's point of view: The right thumb is on the left side, and the right index finger is on the right side of the handle.

In the case of the overlapping grip, the little finger of the right hand rests in the gap between the index and middle finger of the left hand.

The complete grip as viewed from the side.

movement cannot hold the club the same way as a tournament player who is trying to battle a hook. The effectiveness of adjusting your grip has its limits because adjusting the grip does not remedy every problem involving the flight of the ball.

Start with the neutral grip. The Vs of both hands point to the right collarbone The flight path of the ball indicates that this grip does not close the clubface far enough if the ball seems to veer off to the right. In this case, rotate both hands to the right until the Vs point to your right shoulder. When using the neutral grip, if the ball consistently veers to the left, rotate your hands to the left until the Vs point to your chin.

The second way to accommodate individual differences involves the little finger of the right hand. When using the overlapping grip, the little finger of the right hand rests in the gap between the index and middle fingers. Players with very small hands may have trouble with this grip because their little finger may slip out of the gap. If that is the case, they should use the interlocking grip, in which the little fingers interlock. (Jack Nicklaus uses this grip.) This method guarantees that both hands remain securely in place. However, players should make sure that the right hand does not move too far to the right when the little finger of the right hand hooks onto the little finger of the left.

For children, even the interlocking grip is sometimes not enough. We suggest that youngsters use the ten-finger grip (also called the baseball grip), with all fingers touching the handle of the club and the hands as close together as possible.

Complete Grip

The drawings on pages 20–22 show a complete grip from different perspectives. You should always feel that both hands are a unit and are equally involved when swinging the club. Also, make sure that you can easily lift the club off the ground by tilting your wrist towards your thumb. In this lifted position, the angle between your lower arm and the club should be approximately 90 degrees.

Your grip is correct if you can easily lift the club off the ground using only wrist action.

Regardless of whether you are learning the grip from scratch or changing from one you have previously used, the grip will feel awkward in the beginning. Sometimes this causes your hands to tighten up. Try to avoid this because your wrists should move freely when swinging the club.

You have the ideal hold on the handle when the club won't slide out of your hands. The grip always tightens during the swing, eliminating the danger of holding the club too loosely (see also opposite page).

The club rotates in your hands at the moment of impact because the face of the club does not hit the sweet spot, not because you are holding the club too loosely. The swing generates so much force that even if you hold on to the handle tighter, the club rotates anyhow. The intensity of your grip

does not depend on the last three fingers (middle to little finger). Only the index finger and the pad of the little finger of the left hand create the intensity. The club, wedged between the two, rests diagonally on the inside of the hand. The pressure increases automatically due to the steadily increasing force of the pull. Pressure on the left thumb occurs only at the highest point of the backswing. The thumb keeps the club from swinging too far back. The middle and ring fingers of the right hand assert most of the pressure on the club. The thumb and index finger push slightly against each other at the level of the joint of the thumb. These two fingers do not exert force on the club. The little finger rests passively on the left hand during the swing.

The club, wedged between your index finger and the pad of the thumb, can be held without a lot of effort.

Make sure that the grip does not change during the swing. There are three points, often at the top of the backswing, where this grip change might take place:

1. At the point where the pad of the little finger of the left hand touches the handle
2. At the point of contact between the pad of the right thumb and the left thumb
3. At the point where the thumb and index finders of the right hand make contact

In theory, after a successful drive you should be able to use the same grip without making any adjustments. In practice, however, you should loosen the grip between shots to avoid tensing up your hands. Also, every time you loosen your grip you have the opportunity for more practice.

To create a good swing, you should practise your grip every day. You don't need to go to a driving range. Choose one club and practise it at home.

Lifting the pad of your left hand off the handle (above), **loosening the contact between the pad of your right thumb and the left thumb** (left) . . .

. . . and loosening the contact between your index finger and the thumb of your right hand (right). **All three cause the club to swing too far back, forcing you to adjust your grip during the forward swing.**

THE GRIP

- The handle of the club, wedged between the index finger and the pad of the left hand, is mainly held in place by the fingers of the right hand.
- Both Vs point to the right collarbone. The knuckles of two fingers from each hand are visible.
- The pressure on the grip is no greater than that of a handshake.
- The grip should not change during the swing.

When you are standing upright, the end of your club should not touch the ground.

Position and Stance

Position

I am sure many of you have wondered why golfers assume such a strange position when they are about to drive the ball. The reason is not immediately obvious, but if you look a little closer, it will make sense. Try the following experiment:

Take a 6 iron and stand upright, gripping it properly. If you let your arms hang down, you will notice that the club does not even reach the ground.

In other words, in some form or other you must make yourself a little shorter. If you let a beginner follow his instincts, you will see that he bends his back forward until the club reaches the ground.

This is one way of hitting a ball; however, it is impossible to remain in that position when reaching back to start the swing. The position would create far too much tension in the back, and a player who has assumed such a position will tend to "grow taller" while reaching back and (in order to meet the ball) "grow smaller" again when the club moves forward. This maneuver requires a lot of skill and coordination and is not very reliable over the long haul.

As you have seen, one of the many functions of the proper position is to permit the player to be able to rotate the body effectively without having to change his original position.

In addition, a player must allow the upper body to slope forward because the ball is on the ground, and the club must move around the body at an angle.

A player's position must also ensure that he does not lose his balance during the swing.

The club must be on the ground and return to the same place at impact. For this to happen, the player has to have sufficient room between the end of the handle and his thighs because this space decreases as the lower body rotates during the forward swing. In order to assume the ideal position, a player makes himself smaller by adjusting the angle between the knees and the hip joints.

The angle of the knees is the angle formed by the lower legs and thighs. However, golf players do not bend their knees in the conventional sense. Rather,

Beginners are often too timid to bend their knees and hip joints, preferring to bend their backs.

they, as I like to call it, bend their thigh bones. To do this, players bend their knees without pushing them forward. The hips are back far enough so that the hip bones are above the heels. Both patellas are vertically in line with the balls of the feet. Bending the hip joints improves the awkward angle of the hips.

The angle of the hips is the angle created by the upper body and the thighs. After achieving the position discussed above, the player should bend the upper body forward until (seen from the side) the middle of the shoulders is in line with

Golf is not played with "bent knees,"...

... actually, it is the thigh bones that "bend," without noticeably pushing the knees forward.

the knees. The spine is now at a 30 degree angle. The weight of the body should be balanced equally between the heels and the balls of the feet.

Make sure that you do not bend or hollow out your back in this position and don't change the position of your lower body. If it is difficult for you to assume the position, use a mirror to check yourself from the side.

Beginners always insist that this posture is unnatural. Many have difficulty with it because they think they look silly. This is somewhat like sitting on a chair—if you sit with your back really straight, you feel unnatural and uncomfortable. Once you assume a comfortable position, you are in a position that is damaging to your spine.

When playing golf, the correct position is not comfortable. Most players experience a certain tension in the muscles of the lumbar region, indicating that those muscles are not accustomed to being used. This tension will disappear in time. When assuming the correct position, and experiencing the tension in the muscles, you will get a sense of being ready for action, similar to what a sprinter experiences at the starting block.

In order to realize that this position is not all that unnatural, imagine that you want to catch a large golf bag that somebody is dropping into your arms from above. How would

When assuming the correct position, your hip bones are vertically in line with the heels, and the middle of the shoulders is exactly above the patellas and the balls of your feet.

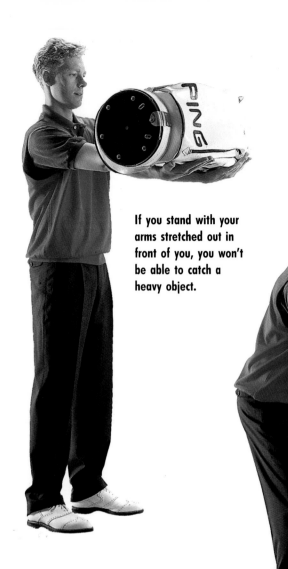

If you stand with your arms stretched out in front of you, you won't be able to catch a heavy object.

However, if you assume an athletic stance, the large muscles in your back and thighs will allow you to succeed.

you instinctively hold your body? Most certainly, you wouldn't stand totally erect with outstretched arms. That position would be fine if the object were light, but a heavier object would fall to the ground because, in this position, your arms would have to carry the whole load. You would most likely assume a more efficient position with your arms much closer to your body. And that is exactly the position we use when playing golf!

What follows is a more detailed discussion of the position of your arms, hands, and the club. In a correct position, your arms should be relaxed and hanging down almost vertically. The upper arms should be in close contact with the upper body,

halfway to the elbows. The distance between your thighs and hands should be as wide as your fist.

If you are standing in the proper position, the entire sole of the club is touching the ground, the weight of your body is equally divided between your heels and the balls of your feet, and the distance to the ball is correct.

When you are in the proper position, your lower arms and club (when viewed from the side) will form an angle. The shorter the club, the larger the angle. You can see this angle reflected in the bend of the wrists towards the side of the little finger (ulnar flexion). Except for this detail, the position for a full swing is the same, no matter which club you use. The distance between the end of the grip and the ground is always the same, regardless of the length of the shaft.

The correct position of the head allows it to become a straight extension of the spine.

Many players bend their head down too far, thinking they have a better view of the ball. But you should keep your head up because your left shoulder must fit under your chin when your body rotates, and the shoulders should not rotate at too steep an angle. When you look at a player from the front, both his eyes should be level. In other words, his head should not tilt to the side. When the head isn't straight, the balance can be off and the starting position of the club can be incorrect.

An example of the proper position as viewed from the side (left). The position is the same for all shots because the distance between the end of the grip (independent of the length of the shaft) and the ground is always the same (right).

Addressing the ball with a medium iron, the player positions his feet shoulder-width apart. When using longer irons, the stance is wider; for shorter irons, the stance is narrower.

For clubs with longer shafts, the stance can be wider; for those that are shorter, the stance can be narrower.

In the ideal stance, the left foot turns out about 25 degrees. The right foot turns out a little less since the lower part of the body rotates somewhat less in the backswing than in the downswing. The knees (when viewed from the front) are vertically in line with the feet.

Because the right hand grips the club lower than the left hand, the right shoulder should also be lower than the left. The result is that the whole upper body is leaning slightly to the right. The weight distribution is approximately 51 percent on the right side and 49 percent on the left. Since the difference is so minimal, most players aren't even aware of it.

The position of the ball depends on the length of the club. A player using a short iron cares more about accuracy than distance. Accuracy increases with backspin, which produces a steady flight, adds to the height of the flight, and controls the distance the ball will roll after it hits the ground. The amount of backspin depends on the angle of the club at impact. The greater the angle, the more backspin the ball has. The closer the ball is to the right foot, the steeper the angle on impact. Thus, when using a short iron (sand wedge to an 8 iron), place the ball in the center between both feet.

When using a wood, you want the ball to travel as far as possible without a lot of backspin, because you want the flight path to be low and the ball to roll as far as possible after it hits the ground.

In the same way, a steep angle at impact reduces the distance a ball travels, since the force behind the clubhead isn't directed at the target.

When using a wood, the ball should be in line with the inside of the heel. That

Stance

To determine the correct width of the stance (the distance between the feet), the player must find a compromise between his ability to rotate the body easily and the best footing. The farther apart the feet are, the more secure the stance, but the more difficult it will be to fully turn the body. For this reason, most golfers keep their feet at shoulder width. Players with more flexibility assume a stance that is a little wider, and less athletic players adopt a somewhat narrower stance. This holds true for medium clubs (5, 6, and 7 irons).

The hands are slightly to the left of the body's center.

The position of the ball depends on the club you use. The farther to the right the ball is, the steeper the angle will be at impact, and the farther to the left the ball, the flatter the angle.

When using a short iron, play the ball from the center of your stance.

With a medium long iron, the ball should be slightly to the left of center.

When using a wood from the tee, the ball should be approximately in line with the inside of your left heel.

way, the club hits the ball at approximately its lowest point in the swing. When using a longer or shorter club, place the ball somewhere between these two positions.

Often teachers advise their students to keep their left arm and the club in one line so that their hands are also in front of the ball at impact. In my opinion, this position is dangerous because the club is too flat during the first part of the swing. I've learned that hand position isn't as important in the downswing as it is during the backswing.

You can find the proper position of the hands in relation to the ball by lining up the ball with the heel and then positioning your hands on the handle of a wood so that the shaft of the club (viewed from the front) is at a right angle to the ground. Your hands will be slightly to the left of the center line of the body and directly above the clubhead, which is behind the ball.

The hand position on the handle is the same for all shots and for every ball. This means that when you use a short iron, your hands are in front of the ball. When using medium to long clubs, your hands are exactly above the ball. When using a wood, your hands are slightly behind the ball. To check on the position of your hands, stick a tee into the hole at the end of the handle. The tee should point towards the left half of your body.

POSITION AND STANCE

- To make yourself "smaller," bend your thighs, keep the back straight, and lean forward from the hips.
- The chin is up, eyes level, and the head not tilted to either side.
- The feet are at shoulder width and point slightly to the outside (the left more so than the right).
- Depending on the choice of club, the ball is directly in the center between your feet (for a short iron) and lines up with the inside of the left heel (for a wood from the tee).
- During address, the hands are slightly to the left of the center of the body.

During practice, always lay a club on the ground midway between the tip of your shoes and the ball, parallel to the intended line to the target.

Preparing for the Shot

Aiming

In golf, aiming is problematic, since you always stand parallel to the intended line to the target with your eyes a good bit away from this direction. In most other sports where you send an object towards a target (like archery or bowling) at least one eye always looks at the target.

The problem, then, for the golfer is to align oneself exactly parallel to the intended line to the target. To do this, he would have to be able to turn the head 90 degrees and try to aim at a point that is the same distance to the left of the target as his feet are from the ball. Finally, the feet must be positioned on the imaginary line that runs parallel to the path to the pin.

However, very few players could accomplish this with one hundred percent accuracy. For example, assuming that the pin is 165 yards (150 m) away and that the distance between a player's feet is 20 inches (50 cm), if a player places one foot just 2 inches (5 cm) too far forward or too far back, he would already be aiming 50 feet (15 m) wide right or the left of the target!

On the course, the player looks for an intermediate target.

Thus, it is impossible to position yourself properly from the side. What follows is the only effective way to aim:

After a test swing, you must stand (as viewed from the target) behind the ball. From this position, search for an intermediate target that is between 8 and 40 inches (20–100 cm) in front of the ball in the intended line to the target. An intermediate goal might be an old divot. After deciding on the intermediate goal, set the club on the ground, placing the clubface so that it lines up with the intended line to the intermediate target. The reason is obvious: It is much easier to aim at a goal that is just a short distance away than to aim at one that is 165 yards (150 m) away.

Lining Up

Point your right foot vertically towards the intended line and direct your eyes from the intermediate target to the real one. Your body is slightly to the left of the target. Next, bring your left foot into its final position, correcting the right foot if necessary. Your body is now exactly parallel to the intended line to the target. A line connecting your shoulders, hips, knees, feet, and lower arms would be parallel to the intended flight of the ball.

The player's body, including the feet, hips, shoulders, and lower arms, is parallel to the intended line to the target.

Look again at the target. Less experienced players often get tense at this point. A good player, however, relaxes. Some players move back and forth on their feet; others move the club up and down or go into a so-called waggle, letting the club dangle from side to side. All of these movements help to break the tension in the lower arms and wrists. Each player has to find his own method of getting ready so that he can be relaxed and still swing with concentration.

Trigger

Golf requires a player to go instantly from the starting position into a flowing, rhythmic movement. In sports such as tennis, soccer and basketball, players are already in motion long before they make contact with the ball. To counter this problem, many golfers choose to initiate their swing with a so-called trigger. A trigger can be any type of movement carried out before swinging the golf club. Some players push their right knee in the direction of the target; others move the club up and down. A "forward press" can also be a trigger. In this case, the hands push a little bit towards the target. However, only use this trigger if you can pull the club back to the proper position.

The fact that the ball is resting motionless on the ground is not necessarily an advantage. A stationary ball can create problems, not the least of which are mental ones. A player has lots of time to think before starting to move the club. Usually the thoughts are about all the things that can go wrong.

The goal is to make sure, before you start your drive, that you are very confident about the sequence of your actions (grip, test swing, aiming, lining up, trigger), so that your swing is always the same. Don't leave time for thinking about mistakes. If your preparations are different every time, you should not be surprised if your swing is different every time.

PREPARING FOR A DRIVE
• For a long drive, line up an intermediate target to make aiming easier.
• Point the head of the club at the intermediate target, then line up your whole body parallel to the line to the target.
• Choose a trigger to use just prior to moving the club so that the beginning of your swing is smoother.

In the preliminary position for lining up, the clubhead points to the intermediate target before the player's feet and body assume their final position.

The shots (hitting, approach, and putting) are not the only things that make golf so interesting. Rather, it is the ability of a player to come to terms with the always unique circumstances of a particular golf course and accept its challenges. This makes the game complete. And when, on top of the game itself, you are presented with the incredible beauty of Mauna-Lani in Hawaii . . .

The SWING

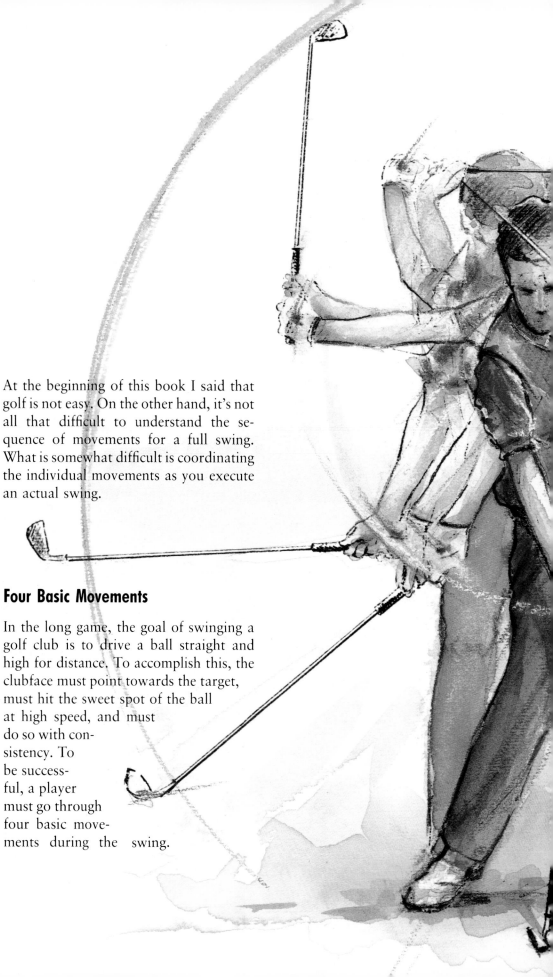

From the backswing to the downswing, the club covers an arc of 270 degrees. Counting the follow-through, the arc is 400 degrees.

At the beginning of this book I said that golf is not easy. On the other hand, it's not all that difficult to understand the sequence of movements for a full swing. What is somewhat difficult is coordinating the individual movements as you execute an actual swing.

Four Basic Movements

In the long game, the goal of swinging a golf club is to drive a ball straight and high for distance. To accomplish this, the clubface must point towards the target, must hit the sweet spot of the ball at high speed, and must do so with consistency. To be successful, a player must go through four basic movements during the swing.

Body Rotation

From the address position, a player must turn around his spine. During the backswing, muscular tension builds between the upper and lower body because the upper body rotates about twice as far as the lower body does.

The energy created by the tension in the muscles is released in the course of the downswing and helps the clubhead gain the necessary speed.

No up or down movements occur during the swing. All parts of the body that are in front of the spine, such as the head and chest, move to the right during the backswing and to the left during the follow-through.

Flexing the Wrists

During the backswing, the wrists flex towards the side of the thumb (radial flexion), and during the downswing, they flex in the direction of the little finger (ulnar flexion). The wrists turn a golf swing into a two-lever system, multiplying many times the force created by the arms and the body. A proper grip is one of the most important parts of this process.

Rotating the Lower Arms

Both lower arms rotate clockwise during the backswing (pronation of the left lower arm, supination of the right) and in the opposite direction during the downswing. This guarantees that the club stays in the proper plane.

Moving the Arms Away from the Body

During the backswing, the arms move up and away from the body. They move down again on the forward movement. The distance between the arms and the body must increase in the second phase of the backswing so that the arms move in the correct plane. Correspondingly, in the downswing, they must move down again while the upper body rotates to the left.

In addition to the four basic movements, many golfers perform other, unnecessary movements. Of course, even

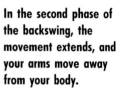

In the second phase of the backswing, the movement extends, and your arms move away from your body.

In the first phase of the backswing, because of the rotation of your body and lower arms and because of a slight flexing of your wrists, the club moves only to the right.

those can contribute to a successful drive, but consistency often suffers. Usually these movements do little but make the swing more complicated. Consistency is what golfers strive for. Almost every player has successful shots, but few produce them on a consistent basis. In other words, don't believe that your swing is correct just because one shot was successful. Your success may just be a coincidence in which several mistakes have cancelled each other out. In addition, it is a fallacy to think that

only bad shots need to be corrected in order to improve your game.

Careful analysis of video tapes shows that all swings look alike, provided that a player is not in a phase in which he is changing his technique. If in the course of several shots, the balls seem to react differently, you might consider whether the same mistake causes different results. Some golfers also make the mistake of believing that their test swings are perfect and that things only go wrong when they have to hit the ball. During test swings, you never know if the club returned exactly to the position from which it started. Also, you learn nothing about the position of the clubface at impact during a practice swing. Both factors, together responsible for the flight path of the ball, can be absolutely wrong during the test swing without the player ever being aware of it.

During the downswing, your body reverses while your arms are moving down. At the moment of impact, your body is back in the address position (the club slightly behind, and your hands slightly in front of the ball).

In order to describe the four basic movements, I have divided the swing into ten separate phases. For the sake of clarity and to make details more vivid, a player posed for the photos. These are snapshots of individual movements and do not represent one continuous swing. However, a golf swing is not a string of individual movements, but rather one flowing sequence of movements. In other words, after you have analyzed your swing and perhaps made some changes, you have to put all the parts back together again.

This chapter is not meant to be a checklist. Instead, use it as a kind of dictionary to find answers to detailed questions that might occur to you while you are learning.

After impact, the club continues to follow through naturally, while your whole weight rests on the outside of the left foot.

Even if the amount of the information that follows seems a bit frightening, remember that you can ignore all those things that you are already doing right. Should you detect a mistake, remember the movement that seems to be the cause and make the necessary correction. After you have corrected the mistake and practised that detail, try to embed it in your subconscious.

Backswing

To refresh your memory, we started this chapter with a photo of the address position. The auxiliary lines in the two drawings on this page represent the plane through which the club is moving (viewed from the side). The length depends on the club used. Here it is a 6 iron. The longer the iron, the flatter the plane.

Phase 1

After you have completed your trigger, move the club backwards without chang-

ing its plane. Using your spine as the axis, rotate your hands, arms, and shoulders (and to a lesser extent your hips) to the right, making sure that the Y shape formed by the arms and the club does not change. Continue the movement until the club has gone just past the 45 degree mark on an imaginary arc. Up to this point, you

The address and club position as seen from the side (left-hand drawing), **and the same position viewed from the front** (photo below).

In the first phase, the club always stays in exactly the same plane in which

it started, as determined by the lie of the club (right-hand drawing). **The Y created by the club and the arms should rotate around your spine to the right without changing its shape** (photo right).

have been using only lateral force. The club reaches its highest and lowest points through its own momentum because the spine, as the center of the rotating movement, is behind the club. A backswing will always be negatively affected when a player tries to pull the club up, across the ground, inside, or when he pulls back to the intended line to the target.

In order to determine if the Y shape has changed in this phase, you can check if the end of the handle and the leading edge of the club are still pointing to the left side of your body as they did in the address position. In addition, the distance between the end of the handle and your body at this point should be the same as in the address position.

The head of the club must line up with the intended line to the target. This is so if the club always moves in the same plane.

Phase 2

In this phase, the wrists and lower arms play an active role in the swing. The wrists flex; the lower arms rotate. In order to check to see if you are executing this part of the swing properly, watch the club. When it is parallel to the ground, it should also be parallel to the intended line of the target. If it is, and if the edge of the left hand is vertically in line with the outside of the right foot, both basic movements (flexing the wrists and rotating the underarms) have been executed perfectly. Up to this point, the end of the handle has only moved to the right.

If, when parallel to the ground, the shaft of the club is pointing to the right of the target, you have either rotated your arms too much or flexed your wrists too late, the way Barry Lane and Bernhard

Langer do. On the other hand, if the underarm rotation was insufficient or the wrists flexed too early (with the club parallel to the ground), the shaft will clearly point past the target on the right side, the way Ronan Rafferty's does.

During the second phase, the rotation of the body also increases, and the head begins to move to the right.

If the shaft of the club is in a position parallel to the ground, it must also be parallel to the intended line to the target (drawing). **With the club parallel to the ground, your wrists should flex when the edge of the left hand is vertically above the outside of the right foot** (photo).

Phase 3

In this phase, the club reaches beyond 90 degrees and is vertical to the ground (when viewed from the front). The four basic movements continue:

1. The hands rise to their highest point during the backswing, pulling the arms away from the body.

    The following example might explain the process: A player can hold a towel under each arm during the address and up to this phase. Since the club is now moving up, the arms will automatically move away from the body, and the towels will fall down. A swing in which the towels do not fall down is much too flat.

2. The greatest change during this movement (when viewed from the front) is obvious in the way the angle between the lower arms and the club changes. This angle is now about 90 degrees, which means that the wrists have turned more in the direction of the thumb.

    The advantage of flexing the wrists early is that you don't have to do so just prior to changing direction in the forward swing, the critical phase of the swing. Of course, flexing is possible even at that point, but the player needs a lot of strength and coordination to do this in a controlled fashion, as Jack Nicklaus and Greg Norman do. However, you should not start too early. The wrists should remain passive so that you can guide the club back to its original position.

3. The lower arms rotate farther so that the end of the club handle points towards the target. Even if in the course of this phase the end of the handle continues to point backwards, the extension of the shaft will always be in line with the intended line to the target.

4. The position of the body has changed little, and only a minimal increase in the rotation takes place.

    Three of the four basic movements of the backswing have already taken place: the movement of the arms away from the body, the rotation of the lower arms, and the radial flexion of the wrists.

The end of the club handle points to the intended line to the target. Your hands are above the plane of the club (drawing). **Your wrists flex far enough for your left arm and the shaft to form a right angle. Your body has rotated about 50 degrees** (photo).

Phase 4

The rotation of the body is most important in the last phase of the backswing. Since the club, hands, and arms are already in the proper relation to the body, you need only concentrate on bringing them through the correct rotation.

The body should turn until the shoulders are at a right angle to the intended line of the target. The hips have rotated 35 to 45 degrees. This turning motion is like a wind-up toy, creating tension that, given the same amount of shoulder rotation, is much greater the less the hips rotate. Novice players try to avoid this tension. Either they don't rotate their shoulders enough, or they rotate their hips too much. You can measure both by the extent to which the left foot comes off the ground. When the body is fully turned, the head will be the width of half a head farther to the right than it was in the address position. Most golfers can't picture this rotating around the spine which is not in the middle of the body. However, the following explanations have been useful:

Instead of one vertical axis running through the center of the body, precluding any sideways movement of the head, imagine that you have two. One is the backswing axis, and the other is the downswing axis. Both run through the bones of the hips. During the backswing, you rotate to the right, during downswing around the left axis. If you should move outside of either axis, the sideways movements will be too strong.

During the backswing, only the upper body moves sideways. The lower part of the body, particularly the right leg, does not move to the right during the backswing. Rather, it serves as support for the upper body. In golf, tension builds up in the back of the thigh muscles of the right leg where part of the energy is stored and then released during the downswing.

Just as in high jumping, golf has an ideal approach length. However, the length of the approach is less important than the speed of the clubhead at impact. To continue with the high-jump analogy: A distance of 100 yards (92 m) gives the jumper no advantage, because the speed at the time of the jump doesn't increase

At the highest point of the swing, the club is parallel to the ground and in line with the intended line to the target. The original position of your body has not changed. Your left arm is parallel to the original plane of the club (drawing). When compared to the address position, your shoulders have rotated 90 degrees, and your head has moved to the right by the width of half a head (photo).

The head of the club moves at an angle corresponding to the lie of the club in the first phase and then increases somewhat. The backswing and downswing are almost identical. Your hands (more precisely the end of the club handle and not the arms) move along a very steep plane since they only move down slightly in the downswing.

when the distance of the approach lengthens. Similarly in golf: The speed of the clubhead doesn't increase when you reach farther back.

Every player must figure out how far back to swing. The answer will depend on how much force he gives the club at the start of the downswing. The greater the force in the beginning, the shorter the backswing should be, and vice versa. In general, a backswing ends at about the point where the shaft of the club has moved to just beyond a 270 degree arc. This is true for longer irons and woods. When using shorter clubs, the backswing is also shorter. The full swing with a

wedge, for instance, has an arc that is just beyond 225 degrees.

Many golfers believe they can solve their problems with the swing by using a slow and short backswing. This will simplify the swing, and mistakes during the sequence of the movements are easier to correct, but the goal should always be to learn the correct sequence of movements. The speed of the movement is less important.

Many discussions center on the position of the left arm during the backswing. I have already mentioned that in the address position the left arm should hang down, long and relaxed. That is also true

The golf course at the Gary Player Country Club in Sun City, South Africa, was designed around holes and not the other way around. Even the lake is artificial.

for the swing. The arm should not become longer or shorter during the backswing because a change would require compensation during the downswing. Don't consciously put your left arm in a fixed position to prevent lengthening. Bending the elbow a little during the backswing is not as bad as sticking it out, because the centrifugal force during the downswing "stretches" your arm down automatically. In fact, during the downswing the club pulls at your arms with a weight of about 90 pounds (40 kg).

At the highest point of the backswing, the dead point, a few details require our attention:

1. The angle between the knee and hip that we talked about in the section on address position remains the same. This means that it is not wider or narrower. Since the rotation of the body creates tension, many players try to avoid the tension by "growing taller" during the backswing. However, then they have to compensate during the downswing, making it difficult to acquire a consistent sequence of movements.

2. The hands and both elbow joints form an approximate equilateral triangle. The left arm is parallel to the plane of the club, the right arm is parallel to the ground, and the lower part of the right arm is parallel to the spine. The angle between the upper right arm and shoulders is approximately 135 degrees. It should never be more, or the arms will come too far away from the body as, for example, Fred Couples' do.

The head of the club and your hands form a wider arc during the backswing than they do during the downswing.

3. Viewed from the side, the clubhead should be between the player's hands and head and should be parallel to the ground in line with the intended line to the target. If the club does not go through a 270 degree arc, the shaft of the club must point slightly left to the target. If the player reaches beyond the horizontal plane, the shaft must point more to the right. The leading edge of the club is still parallel to the lower left arm. If the club points too far into the air, it is too closed; if pointing forward, it is too open. In either case, make sure that you check the grip, the flexion of the wrists (in the direction of the back or the palm of your hand), and the plane your arms move in. These are where you'll find the reason for an unnatural clubface position.

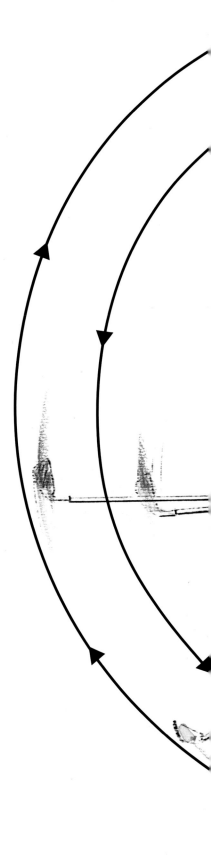

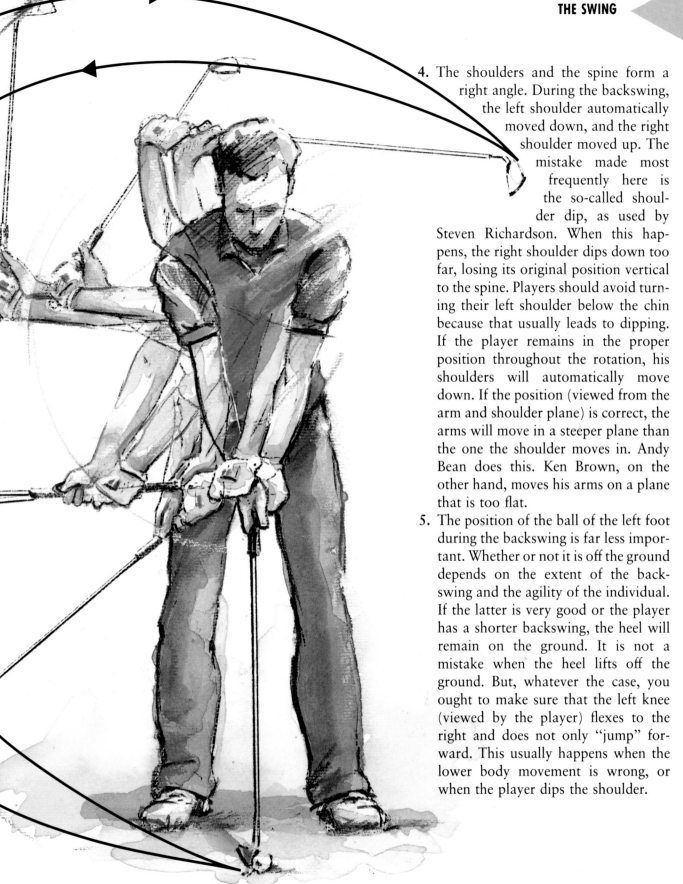

4. The shoulders and the spine form a right angle. During the backswing, the left shoulder automatically moved down, and the right shoulder moved up. The mistake made most frequently here is the so-called shoulder dip, as used by Steven Richardson. When this happens, the right shoulder dips down too far, losing its original position vertical to the spine. Players should avoid turning their left shoulder below the chin because that usually leads to dipping. If the player remains in the proper position throughout the rotation, his shoulders will automatically move down. If the position (viewed from the arm and shoulder plane) is correct, the arms will move in a steeper plane than the one the shoulder moves in. Andy Bean does this. Ken Brown, on the other hand, moves his arms on a plane that is too flat.

5. The position of the ball of the left foot during the backswing is far less important. Whether or not it is off the ground depends on the extent of the backswing and the agility of the individual. If the latter is very good or the player has a shorter backswing, the heel will remain on the ground. It is not a mistake when the heel lifts off the ground. But, whatever the case, you ought to make sure that the left knee (viewed by the player) flexes to the right and does not only "jump" forward. This usually happens when the lower body movement is wrong, or when the player dips the shoulder.

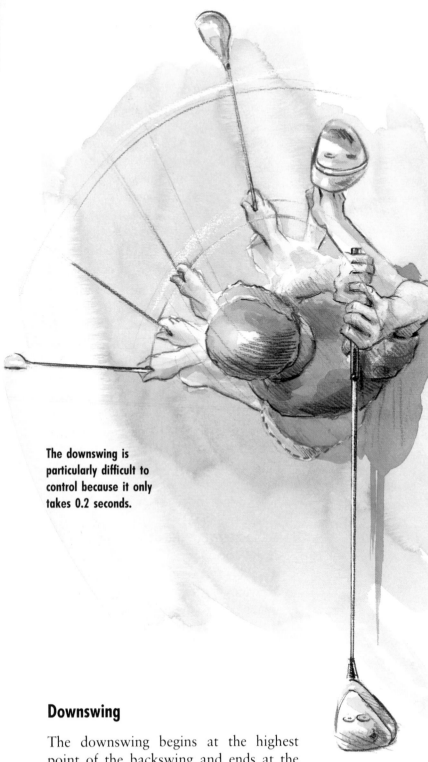

The downswing is particularly difficult to control because it only takes 0.2 seconds.

Downswing

The downswing begins at the highest point of the backswing and ends at the point of impact.

You need to know that the downswing is not the symmetrical opposite of the backswing. Not only is the position of the club at the moment of impact clearly different from that at address, but the individual movements throughout are also different. On the other hand, you can't totally separate the backswing from the downswing because there is no pause between the two. In fact, there is a moment when the club is still in the backswing motion, but the lower part of the player's body is already moving in the direction of the target.

The four basic movements of the backswing also apply to the downswing, only in reverse order. Support comes from the centrifugal force which aids the release of the flexion of the wrists (ulnar flexion) and the rotation of the lower arms. Generally speaking, the player does not need to pay attention to either movement. What remains are the rotation of the body and the movement of the arms back towards the body.

During the backswing, the lower part of the body follows that of the upper body; this sequence reverses during the downswing.

Phase 5

The first part of the downswing requires the simultaneous movement of the left knee, left arm, and hip. The left knee and the left hip move towards the left, while the hands move down and towards the position they assume at impact. The lower part of the body begins its rotation immediately after the initial lateral movement of the lower body. This causes the upper body to begin rotating in the opposite direction. The shoulders only catch up with the hips after the moment of impact. That is the reason why the upper body (when viewed from the front) appears to dip slightly to the right during the downswing.

For the same reason, the right shoulder is almost always somewhat lower during the downswing than during the backswing.

The downward movement of the hands (centrifugal force automatically pulls them to the outside) assures that the arms begin to make closer contact with the body. The space between the hands and the right shoulder has to become increasingly wider. In most cases, golfers who have pull or slice problems raise their arms much too slowly during this phase of

The distance between your hands and right shoulder is larger than it was at the highest point of the backswing. The angle formed by your left wrist and lower arm begins to dissolve again.

The end of the club handle points to the target. Your hands are still slightly above the original plane of the club.

the backswing. The angle between the left arm and the club (viewed from the front) becomes smaller during the first phase of the backswing due to the slow speed of the clubhead.

The average player cannot duplicate late hitting, a common trait in top golfers. Opening up the angle between the lower arm and the shaft at the right time requires a lot of strength and coordination. The art of the downswing lies in the golfer's ability to coordinate the movements of his body on one side, and that of his arms, hands, and the club on the other.

A strong player usually has much more trouble with movements that are too fast, in other words, closing the clubface early. The result is that the ball pulls to the left. In contrast, the hands of a weaker player can't quite follow the fast rotation of the body, particularly that of the upper body. At the moment of impact, the clubface will be too open, causing the ball to pull to the right. It would be wrong for such a player to hesitate at impact, opening the angle between the club and his arms.

During the subsequent phase of the downswing, the right elbow is considerably lower than the left elbow, bringing the club into a plane that is less steep, compared to the backswing position. The reason is the slight "dip-to-the-right" of the upper body caused by the movement of the lower body, which is somewhat "in front." All this is necessary if the club is to hit the ball from the inside and not lose its alignment with the intended line to the target, as is the case with all "pull-slicers."

The hips are now almost parallel to the intended line to the target, and the weight is still primarily over the right foot. Once a player starts his downswing in such a fashion, the movements during the following phases happen almost automatically.

The club is again parallel to the ground and the intended line to the target, its original position (drawing). The rotation of the shoulders is still less than that of the hips, pointing slightly to the right of the target. The upper body is almost back to the address position.

Phase 6

During this phase, the lower body continues its rotation, and the upper body follows. The shoulders are almost parallel to the intended line to the target.

Now the angle of the right elbow also changes, increasing the space between the hands and the right shoulder. The position of the club is again parallel to the ground and the intended line to the target, just as it was at the beginning of the backswing. If the position is too flat, the club will swing through the ball from outside-to-in or inside-to-out, respectively.

Phase 7

During the seventh phase, just prior to the moment of impact, the wrists flex towards the little finger (ulnar flexion), and the lower arms rotate counterclockwise.

At the moment of impact (viewed from the side), the shoulders point to the left of the target, between 0 degrees for the handicap golfer and 15 degrees for the top golfer. The reason for the difference is that a handicap golfer, who is more likely to battle slicing, must make sure that his arms, hands, and the club move forward early enough; a strong player, who is more likely to battle the hook, must make sure that his body rotates fast enough.

When we view a player from the front, we can make a few comparisons between the position at the moment of impact and that in the address:

The upper body dips slightly to the right, since the head is in the same position as it was in the address position. The lower body, because of the rotation and lateral motion, is farther to the left when compared to the address position. The back of the left hand and the lower arm are in a straight line. The flexion of the left wrist in the direction of the back of the hand, which permits this, happened during the last phase of the swing. This position relates to the fact that the hands are, unlike in the address position (viewed from the target), in front of the ball, allowing the player to swing down and "through" the ball.

During this phase, everything must happen automatically. A player must not try to consciously exert any additional force, which would only slow down the process. A similar situation exists when someone pushes the front wheel of an upside-down bicycle a second time, hoping to make the wheel turn as fast as possible. Because a certain force of energy is already in mo-

tion, the wheel cannot be made to run faster by giving it another push. This is called the principle of freewheeling.

According to scientific research, the speed of the hands must decrease during the second phase of the downswing at the moment when the angle between the left arm and the club (viewed from the front) again increases. The decrease in speed permits maximum force behind the clubhead.

This contradicts the widely held belief

The hands are slightly in front of the ball at the moment of impact, and the head is back in its natural position (photo). **At the moment of impact, the club returns to its original position. The hips point slightly to the left of the target; while the shoulders point directly at the target** (drawing).

that the amount of energy during the downswing must be steadily increased from the beginning to the moment of impact, or even, as has also been suggested, that the increase not begin until the second half of the downswing.

Since very few golfers understand how a ball flies through the air, let me explain it here.

A golfer does not need special techniques to hit the ball in the air. In other words, he does not need to "spoon" the ball into the air. He does not need to worry that at the moment of impact his hands be moving upwards in order to artificially tilt the face of the club. This has to do with the fact that clubfaces already have an angle of between 11 and 16 degrees.

When the player is hitting correctly, the clubface moves down, resulting in a much cleaner hit, particularly when the ball is in poor position. A player does not need to hit under the ball; instead, he plays from above, down, and through the ball. Too many players don't understand the process and try to "spoon" the ball. This is a mistake, particularly in high, short approach shots.

The principle of "hitting down" is correct except for putting and teeing off.

Depending on where the ball lies, the clubhead produces different-size divots on the downswing. The farther to the right the ball is, the shorter the club, and the deeper the divot. With a long iron or wood, the clubhead only brushes the grass.

Many people wonder about the large divots that professional players produce. But even if a deep divot is not the ideal, it is still better than none at all.

The next time you watch a tournament on TV, pay special attention to how those balls that have been hit with a "lot of

grass" react. They usually stop dead immediately after they hit the ground, sometimes even rolling backwards. The vertical angle at impact is not the only factor; others are your equipment (club and ball) and the speed of the clubhead at impact. A clean hit is also important. Together with the loft of the club, these factors influence how quickly a ball will roll backwards. This movement assures that the ball will stop quickly after it hits the ground and renders the ball less sensitive to sidespins. In addition, it gives the ball a more stable flight with an optimal flight curve.

How do you hit the ball from below? If the club meets the ball correctly from the inside, and the player does not attempt to "spoon" the ball into the air, the player's hands at impact will automatically be in front of the ball, and the club will swing downwards. (A club coming in too far on the inside won't hit through the ball from above.)

Follow-Through

The follow-through is the phase that begins after the club has hit the ball.

Some new players question the importance of a phase that starts after the ball has been hit. They believe that nothing can influence the flight path after the ball has been hit.

But that is not correct. For instance, the end point of the swing does impact on the downswing. You can experiment by hitting a few practice shots. Try to change the end position for each swing. You will see that all the forward movements (downswing and follow-through) change, influencing the flight path of the ball. Compared with changing your backswing and downswing, it is relatively easy to change your follow-through and end position.

However, most follow-through problems originate in mistakes made during the backswing: in posture, stance, and even in the grip. Correct those mistakes before you attempt to improve your follow-through.

Most of all, try not to steer the club towards the target during and after impact. This is contrary to the principle of freewheeling and slows down the club before impact. Additionally, it very seldom works.

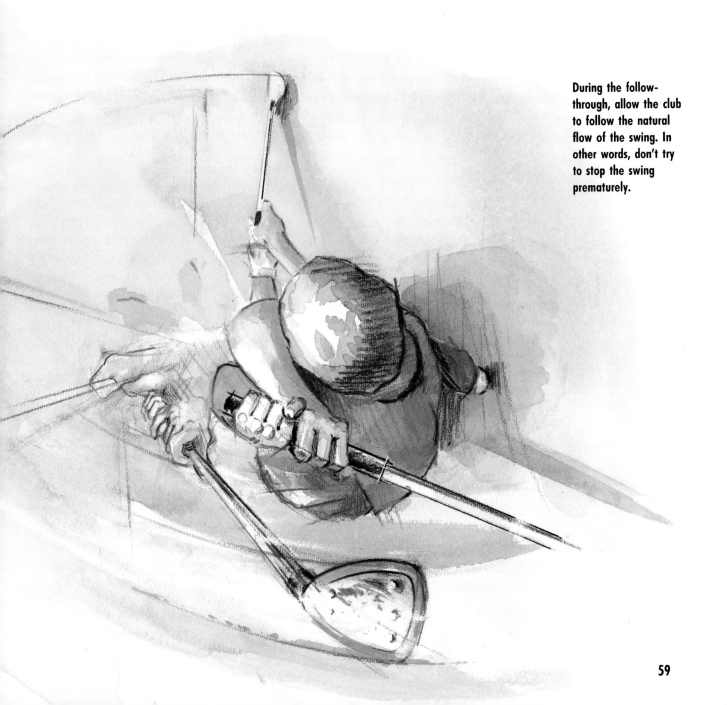

During the follow-through, allow the club to follow the natural flow of the swing. In other words, don't try to stop the swing prematurely.

The club is still in its original plane, since the lower arm does not rotate purposely at the moment of impact.

Phase 8

If the ball were not in the way of the swinging club, the point when the club-head reached its highest speed would be to the left of the impact point (as viewed by the player), the point when both arms extend fully.

The left arm and the club (viewed from the side) align in a straight line. In other words, not until this point does the angle between the club and the shaft of the club dissolve.

Since the shaft of the club (viewed from the side) is back in its original position, the hands are again to the inside (to the left) of the clubhead, as in Phase 1.

Phase 9

During this phase, the end of the handle of the club is closer to the ground than its head, which is in line with the intended line to

The left arm and the shaft of the club form one straight line. The head is rotated so that the player can follow the ball after impact.

the target. The upper body and the lower body are in line again. The belt buckle and the chest bone are pointing slightly to the right of the target. The right arm is parallel to the ground. During the follow-through, the left elbow flexes, and the right arm remains straight—the reverse of the back-swing, where the left arm remains straight and the right elbow flexes.

The body is already in line with its left axis; the player's weight is completely on the outside of the left foot. During Phase 9, the head follows the rotation of the body, making it possible for the player to have a total view of the ball. There is no advantage to keeping your eyes on the spot where the ball was. On the contrary, it is impossible to execute a free-flowing follow-through if your head remains down for an unnecessarily long time. In my opinion, the fear of topping the ball (caused by following the ball with your eyes too early) is not justified. I have never seen a golf player who, in fact, did this. In addition, you can place excessive strain on your spine by keeping your head down too long. Even if your head begins to turn after the club hits the ball, your body (viewed from the side) is still in its original tilt. At this point, your head has not moved up yet. In order to relieve the extra strain on your spine, your body will become upright again during the course of the continuous movement.

Phase 10

During the last phase of the follow-through, the player simply allows the momentum of the club and the arms to take its course. The upper body follows the movement until the belt buckle points slightly to the left of the target and the right shoulder is closer to the target than the left. The upper body is almost upright. The accompanying photo shows the

player totally upright. It is too bad that some teachers ask their students and beginners to tilt the upper body back during this phase. For the uneducated, this motion might look very athletic, but unfortunately, it ensures that the club does not move downwards sufficiently during impact. In addition, it also creates a hollow back, or reverse C, which might injure the spine. The right arm (viewed from the side) is now parallel to the original plane of the club. The hands are at the left side of the head, and the club points away

from the target, since the upper body has straightened up slightly.

During the last two phases, the back of the left hand and the lower arm are in the same position as they were in the address position.

Because of the rotation of the lower body, the right foot only touches the ground at the tip; the left foot has contact with the ground only at the heel and the outside. The knees are close together.

The end of the handle points to the target again. The hands are slightly above the original plane of the club. Straightening up relieves the back.

Upper and lower body have now rotated equally. The eyes are looking at the ball. The upper body is exactly in line with the right leg. Only the tip of the right foot touches the ground.

Learning How to Swing

Some people might think that we have been unnecessarily analytical in this chapter. After all, people are not robots, producing specific angles and positions with one-hundred-percent accuracy. But since our goal is not for you to hit a ball to a certain exact spot, as is the case with "Iron Byron," some deviation is allowed. The positions described are guidelines. However, don't forget that golf clubs and golf balls always follow the law of mechanics. Violations of these laws have consequences.

Many golfers give up trying to learn how to swing a golf club correctly after they have changed their swing and their shots still turn out badly. They think that the correction they made was wrong.

It is incorrect to think a good shot is due to a good swing or that a bad shot is due to a bad swing. In some cases, two mistakes might cancel each other out.

When you first attempt to improve your swing, try not to pay too much attention to hitting the ball correctly. Put the emphasis on the correct execution of the swing.

Bernhard Langer demonstrates here a very good position at the end of the back-swing: . . .

. . . The angles of his body have changed, his arms are higher than his shoulders, and the club is pointing to the target.

Principle of Exaggeration

When I give lessons, I constantly run into the following phenomenon: After analyzing the video we made, a student recognizes his problems and is ready to make the necessary corrections. After only a few tries, he is sure that he has mastered the completely new movement. He is very surprised when I tell him that (viewed with the naked eye) his "new" swing does not look any different from his old one.

An example shows that you shouldn't trust your feelings alone: Imagine that you are driving your car on a highway with little traffic for a long period of time. Suddenly signs alert you to a construction site up ahead and you slow down. Your new speed appears to be extremely slow.

Another scenario: You are driving in the city, and you end up in a traffic jam. After a while, you reach a highway where you can and do accelerate. Your new speed seems very fast, but in fact is no different from the "slower speed" you were driving in the first scenario.

The same holds true for golf: If you have had a very flat backswing in the past, a steeper backswing seems to be extreme; if your swing was too steep, you will think that a neutral swing is too flat.

Since very few golfers are aware of this phenomenon, most golfers usually take steps in the right direction, but their steps are too small.

My students often hear me say, "Exaggerate when you do the exercises and instructions I give you." When a student views the video of his practice session, in which he thinks he has way overdone it, he recognizes that his feelings have deceived him, his swing is just about what it should be.

I cannot emphasize enough the importance of this "exaggeration," and I want you to understand that you are not the exception. Don't trust your feelings. Use a golf teacher, a video camera, a mirror, or a friend to help you see what you are really doing.

As soon as you understand this principle and use it, you can successfully change your swing.

THE GOLF SWING

- Four basic movements have to be executed for the club to be in the correct position at the conclusion of the backswing: rotating the body, flexing the wrists, rotating the lower arms, and moving the arms away from the body. During the downswing, there are only two movements: the arms move closer to the body again and the body rotates to the left, rotating the hips and moving the arms down.
- Either the end of the handle or the clubhead should always point to the target. If the club is parallel to the ground, it should always point to the intended line to the target.
- In the address position, the body rotates around the spine.
- During the backswing, the lower part of the body follows the rotation of the upper body; during the downswing the sequence reverses.

Roon the Ben, Bruce's Castle, Lang Whang, Ca Canny—unusual names for extraordinary driving ranges on the Ailsa Golf Course, a typical championship course for left-handers in Turnberry on the west coast of Scotland, three times scene of the British Open. The light tower in the background is the symbol of the course and part of the club's coat of arms.

MISTAKES and How to CORRECT THEM

Now you know what an ideal golf swing should look like, but you still won't be able to determine in which phase your technique deviates from the ideal.

A weekend golfer can't hope to achieve the perfect swing, one that withstands every pressure. Yet, sometimes adjusting just one movement can enable a player to reach consistency in his game. Most players usually have one specific problem. For instance, the ball consistently veers off to the right, shots with woods are underutilized, irons get topped, etc. This chapter attempts to help you with such problems.

First, however, you must analyze the flight path of the ball. You don't accomplish anything when you complain that nothing works anymore. When asked about the problem, the student usually answers, "I simply can't hit the ball." Telling a golf instructor this is like telling your doctor that you don't feel well.

If you want to solve your problem by yourself, which is certainly possible, you must know exactly what the ball is doing, because aside from the divot, the ball is the only thing that you can see.

After a bad shot, golfers often turn away in disgust and simply continue hitting the ball without looking at what the ball is doing. On the other hand, after a good shot, they will stand motionless for a few seconds, delighting in the flight of their ball.

A player can deduce what the club did at impact from the way the ball behaves. This brings us to the factors that influence the movements at the moment of impact and what a player who wants to improve his game needs to know about them.

In order to recognize how far your swing deviates from the ideal at the moment of impact, you must be able to analyze and interpret the flight of the ball. Only then can you draw conclusions about the movements you are making.

Factors Influencing the Moment of Impact

The half a millisecond when the club makes contact with the ball determines how and where the ball will fly. In all, six factors influence that moment.

Hitting the Ball with the Sweet Spot

In those rare circumstances when a hit feels light, and you hear the perfect thud, the clubhead has hit the ball with the so-called sweet spot.

If you hit a ball with any other part of the clubhead, the ball won't go as far because at the moment of impact the club rotated in your hands. You know this has happened because your hands are not in the same position on the handle as they were before the impact.

If the club rotates to the left (closed), the heel hits the ball. If the club rotates to the right (opened), the tip of the clubhead hits the ball.

The fact that the club rotated in your hands has nothing to do with your grip not being tight enough. In fact, the club always rotates if the ball has not been hit with the sweet spot. Balls hit with the tip of the clubhead usually turn to the right, but if the clubface was rotated to the left, the ball turns to the left. Sockets, or shanks, with an iron also go to the right (only in extreme cases do they go to the left). With a wood, they go to the left. In addition, when a wood is used, the ball will get a right spin when hit with the heel and a left spin when hit with the tip. For this reason, the clubface of a wood has a horizontal bulge. This bulge causes the ball to start out to the left when hit with the heel, compensating for the right spin; a ball starts out to the right when hit with the tip, compensating for the left spin.

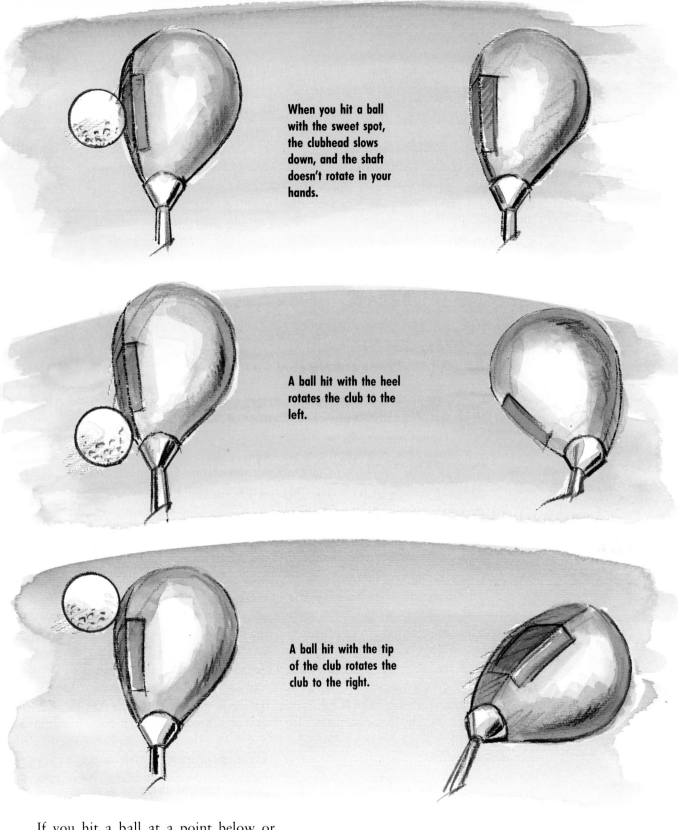

When you hit a ball with the sweet spot, the clubhead slows down, and the shaft doesn't rotate in your hands.

A ball hit with the heel rotates the club to the left.

A ball hit with the tip of the club rotates the club to the right.

If you hit a ball at a point below or above the sweet spot, the ball will not fly the optimal distance nor reach the optimal height.

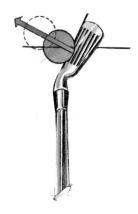

Speed of the Clubhead at the Moment of Impact

This speed determines how far the ball will travel in the air. However, at this point, high speed does not necessarily guarantee a long flight. As we have just discussed, the ball must be hit with the sweet spot for the speed to be transferred, giving the ball the maximum flight. In addition, the angle of the clubhead at the moment of impact and the position of the clubface must also be correct.

Position of the Clubface at the Moment of Impact

At the moment of impact, the clubface can rotate to the right or left of the intended line to the target. If the clubface is not at a right angle to the direction in which the club is moving—the horizontal impact angle—the ball receives a lateral backspin and will not fly straight; instead, depending on the angle of impact, the ball will curve to the left or right while in flight.

Also, the ball will not start out in the direction in which the club is moving; here, too, depending on the speed of the clubhead, the direction of the ball depends on the position of the clubface.

When you use a wood, the ball starts somewhere between where the clubface is pointing and the direction in which the club is moving. In this case, the position of the clubface is the major influence on the direction of the ball. If the swing moves by about 15 degrees, from inside-to-out, and the clubface points in the direction of the intended line to the target, the ball will start out about 5 degrees to the right and then curve to the left for the rest of the flight. The position of the clubface is the deciding factor in which direction the ball will move. In addition, it also influences the height of the trajectory. If the face rotates to the right, the ball will travel a

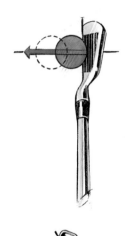

The position of the clubface is a determining factor in the flight path of the ball. At the moment of impact, it can be rotated either to the right (top), or the left (bottom), or vertically to the intended target (middle).

higher but shorter distance and not roll as much. If, on the other hand, the ball curves to the left, the trajectory will be flatter, and the ball will roll farther.

Horizontal Angle at Impact

The angle between the intended line of flight and the horizontal component of the path of the club at the time of impact is the horizontal angle at impact. You can only recognize it when you view it from the side. At the point of impact, the club can move across the intended line to the target (inside in), to the right (inside-to-out), or to the left (outside-to-in). The ball will start in the direction the club is moving, assuming that the clubhead is vertical to the intended line of the target. The pull (a straight ball travelling to the right of the intended line to the target) and the push (a straight ball travelling to the left of the intended line to the target) are usually the result of the wrong horizontal angle at impact. However, when it comes to the direction a ball takes, the horizontal angle at impact is not nearly as important as the position of the clubface.

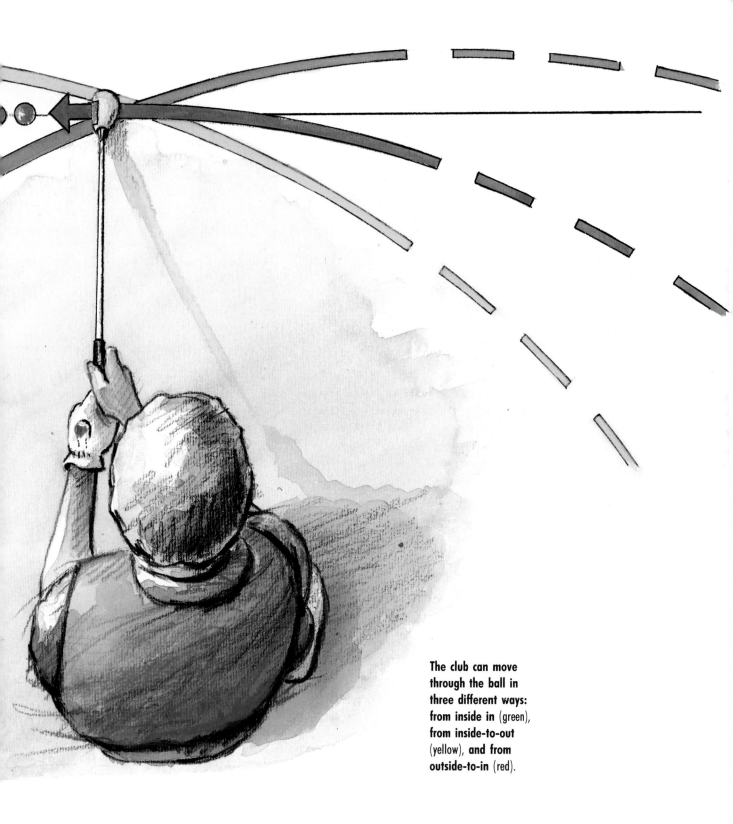

The club can move through the ball in three different ways: from inside in (green), from inside-to-out (yellow), and from outside-to-in (red).

Vertical Angle at Impact

The angle between the ground and the vertical component of the path of the club at impact is called the vertical angle of impact. It can only be observed from the front. It influences the force of the backspin as well as the vertical angle of the ball and the height of the trajectory.

The club can move parallel to the ground at the moment of impact and can hit the ball at either a low or a steep angle. When using a wood, the ideal position of the club is parallel to the ground. When using an iron in the fairway, the club should move slightly downwards, hitting the ball at a steeper angle.

Club Lie at the Moment of Impact

The angle between the shaft of the club and the ground is one factor that has been neglected in the past. In an ideal situation, the sole of the clubhead would be parallel to the ground. If the heel is in the air, which happens all the time when you hit long drives, the ball will curve to the right, even if you don't tilt the clubface laterally, because the loft (the tilt of the clubface) causes the club to hit the ball more on its left side.

A club can move through a ball three different ways: parallel to the ground (top), on the upswing (middle), or on the downswing (bottom).

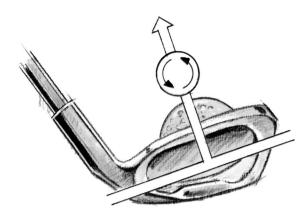

The La Qinta Golf Course on the Costa del Sol in Spain is in the mountains above the town of Marbella. In 1985, pros played the World Cup on this par 71 course.

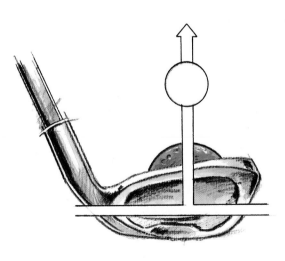

If the heel of the club-head is in the air at the moment of impact, the ball will move to the right and continue to veer even farther to the right (right). If the tip of the clubhead is in the air, the ball starts out moving slightly to the left and continues to veer even farther to the left (far left). Therefore, the lower edge of the clubface should be parallel to the ground (left).

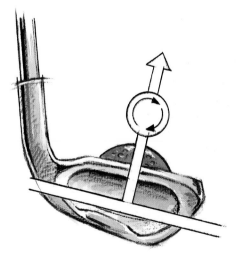

Reasons for Missing the Sweet Spot

In order to understand the aerodynamics of a ball in flight and to correct the most common mistakes, a player must first understand the reasons why the sweet spot is missed at the moment of impact.

Hitting with the Heel or the Tip

The main reason for missing the sweet spot is that either the club or the arms are moving on the wrong plane. If either one of them is too flat, the clubhead moves out in front, on the downswing, and the club hits with the heel. If either one of them is too steep, the clubhead stays behind, and the club hits with the tip.

Another reason the club hits with the heel or the tip is a tilted clubface. When it tilts to the right, the heel is closer to the ball; when it tilts to the left, the tip is closer to the ball. Both situations make it impossible to hit the ball with the sweet spot. The wrong horizontal angle at impact (the club swings through the ball either extremely outside-to-in or inside-to-out) can also be responsible for missing the sweet spot.

Clubhead Speed Either Too Slow or Too Fast

A slow clubhead speed results from several technical factors. First of all, you must establish an angle between your left arm and the club (radial flexion) during the backswing. Without an angle, only your left arm can serve as a lever (left arm together with the club). If, however, you use your wrists as hinges, you have created a two-hinge system that allows you to increase the speed considerably. The angle

If your arm moves in a plane that is too flat, the heel of the club-head hits the ball, leading to hooking and topping (shots with too little ground).

If your arm moves in a plane that is too steep, the tip of the clubhead hits the ball, causing the ball to veer to the right (too much ground).

The following exercise will be helpful if your arm moves on a flat plane: Place your feet together and make a three-quarter swing. Since in such a closed stance your body would be thrown off balance immediately when your arms swing back, they will automatically move in a more level plane.

at the highest point of the swing should be at least 90 degrees. To be most effective, it should not be reduced too early or the club will reach its highest speed before impact. However, keep in mind that late hitting requires much energy and coordination. For most players, attempting to hold back prevents the angle from dissolving at the moment of impact and leaves the clubface open. This, in turn, leads to slicing problems that markedly reduce the distance a ball travels. A player with slicing problems should not attempt to become a late hitter.

The important factors for producing the clubhead speed are: total shoulder rotation of at least 90 degrees with no more than a 45 degree hip rotation and arms following a complete arc of close to 180 degrees. Just as important is the correct shifting of the body's weight: during the backswing on the right foot, during the downswing on the left foot. In addition to proper techniques, physical condition also plays a role. Flexibility, speed, and energy are all important, as is proper equipment. For instance, a shaft that is too stiff or too heavy can markedly reduce the distance of a drive. For most players, the speed of the clubhead alone would be sufficient for driving a ball farther than it often does. The reason a drive falls short of what a player expects is that the player hit the ball badly. Too much clubhead speed during the approach or putting is usually the result of an exaggerated backswing or too much flexing of the wrists.

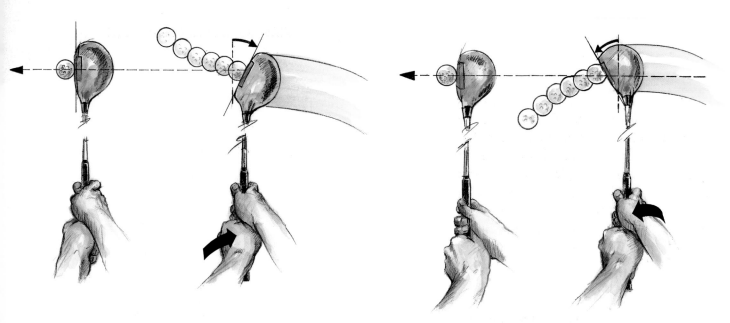

If your hands are too far to the left at address, the clubface will tilt to the right (slice) at impact (left above). **If your hands are too far to the right, the clubface will tilt to the left (hook) at impact** (right above).

The position of your left wrist influences the clubface. Volar flexion: closed (tilted to the left) (left); dorsal flexion: open (tilted to the right) (middle); almost straight: straight (right).

Tilting the Clubface

The most important influence on the position of the clubface is the grip. If your hands turn too far to the left or the right in the address position, the clubface will tilt to the left or the right at the moment of impact because, during the downswing, your hands automatically return to their original position.

The position of the left wrist during the swing can also cause a tilted clubface. If the wrist flexes in the direction of the back of your hand (dorsel flexion), the clubface tilts to the right (open); if it flexes in the direction of the palm of your hand (volar flexion), the clubface tilts to the left (closed). Therefore, during the highest point of the backswing, make sure that your wrists and lower arm are almost in a straight line.

The horizontal angle of impact is another reason a clubface doesn't hit the ball squarely. In most cases, the clubface won't be closed enough when the club approaches the ball from an angle that is too steep, and it isn't open enough when the angle of approach is too flat (from the inside). The section on the horizontal angle at impact discusses the reasons for these mistakes.

If, in relation to the head of the club, the end of the grip is too far in front of or too far behind the ball at impact, the club will be either open or closed when it reaches the ball. The player has hit too early (closed club) or too late (open club). It's also possible that the position of the body at the moment of impact was not correct. If the ball is too far forward, the club is usually open; if, on the other hand, the ball is too far behind, the club is usually closed.

Two other reasons for an open clubface at impact involve body movements. During the backswing, the clubface does not close enough if the player has not shifted his weight sufficiently to the right foot. Not shifting to the right leads the body to move to the left, which inevitably happens during the downswing. As a result, the body and the end of the grip are too far to the left of the ball at impact. This position always produces an open clubface. Leaning to the left during the backswing also causes a problem. The left shoulder is too low because, during the backswing, the upper body leans forward, and the arms move on a steeper plane. When these movements take place during the backswing, the player automatically compensates on the downswing, causing the right shoulder to be too low, and the arms and club then interfere with hitting through the ball (right elbow lower than the left). You can deal with this problem by practising baseball swings which put more emphasis on lower-arm rotation and less on vertical body movements.

If your arms, hands, and club move faster than your body during the downswing (early hitting), the balls will veer to the left (above).

When the rotation of your body is ahead of the forward movement of your arms and the flexion of your wrists, the result is slicing.

In order to make it easier for the club to get to the ball more from the inside than from the outside, pull your right shoulder back a little.

Hitting from the Inside or Outside

In general, a club swings in the direction it assumed at the height of the backswing, provided that the club is parallel to the ground at this point. If it is pointing to the left (flattened at its highest point), the club will most likely move through the ball outside-to-in. If the club is pointing to the right, it will move inside-to-out.

The position of the shoulder can also give some information about where the club moves during the swing. The more open (pointing to the left) the shoulder is

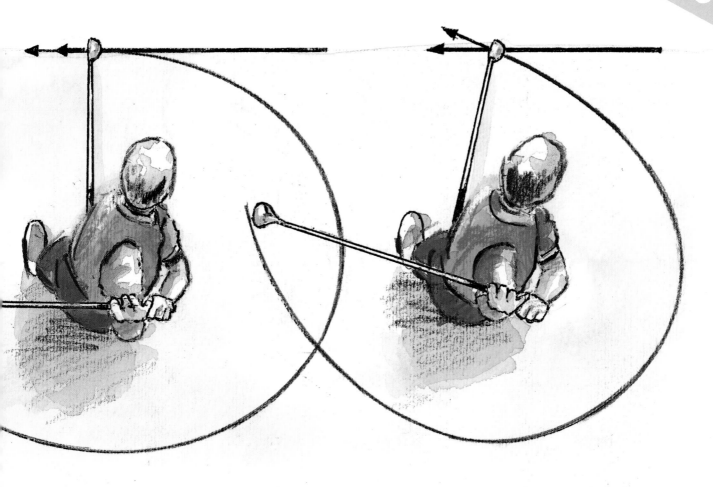

If the club points to the left at the top of the swing (left drawing), **the club will move from the outside-to-in; if it points to the right** (right), **the club will move from the inside-to-out. Therefore, the club should always point squarely at the target** (middle).

at the moment of impact, the more likely it is that the club will move outside-to-in and vice versa, because if the shoulders rotate too little or too much, the hands and usually the clubhead are too far forward or too far back.

To correct a faulty horizontal angle of impact, check the position of your shoulders in the address position. For instance, if your shoulders point to the left, which can be the case if the ball lies too far to the left, the club will probably move through the ball outside-to-in. If your shoulders turn more to the right, the club will probably swing through the ball inside-to-out. In most cases, however, a faulty horizontal angle of impact is the result of a tilted clubface. When the clubface points to the right at the moment of impact, most players instinctively react by trying to move through the ball outside-to-in, and the ball starts out going more to the left.

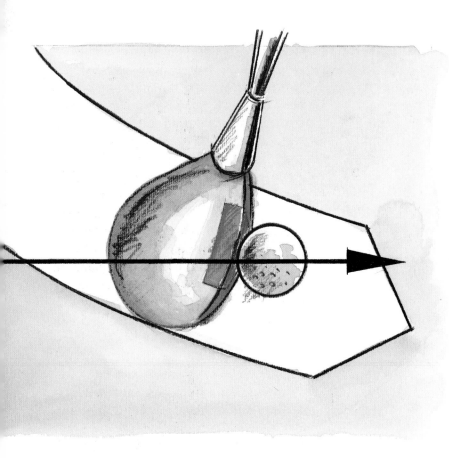

Angle at Impact Too Flat or Too Steep

In general, the club hits the ball at an angle that is too flat or too steep because the horizontal angle at impact was wrong. If the club hits the ball from the outside, the angle is too steep; if the club comes from the inside, the angle is too flat.

Assuming that the club is moving squarely in the direction of the target, the factors contributing to an incorrect horizontal angle at impact are: The body's center of gravity at impact is too far to the right, causing the club to approach the ball at a steep angle; or the center of gravity is too far to the left, causing the club to approach the ball at an angle that is too flat.

The lie of the ball also influences the vertical angle at impact. The farther to the left the ball is, the flatter the angle of the club approaching the ball; the more to the right, the steeper the angle. Flexing the wrists too early, together with a dorsal flexion of the left wrist during the downswing, will flatten the angle at which the club approaches the ball. This happens when you "spoon" the ball into the air. If you flex too late, the angle of approach is

If your forward swing moves from the inside out, the club will usually approach the ball on a flat angle.

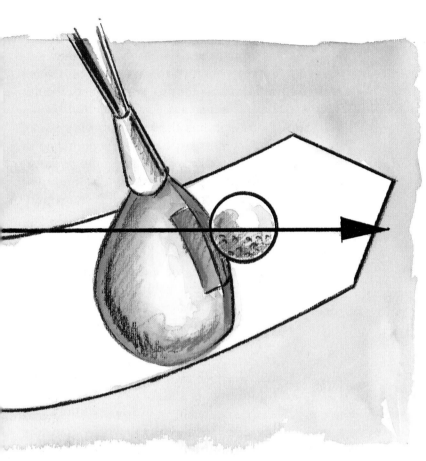

If your club crosses the intended line to the target from the outside in, it will always hit the ball on a steep vertical angle on impact.

steeper. Early flexion usually occurs when the right hand moves away from the grip and the left hand at the highest point of the backswing. The result is that the grip tightens again during the downswing, which leads to a throwing motion, an early hit, and a flat vertical angle at impact. In addition to keeping your right hand in place during the swing, you should make sure that you don't overemphasize your wrists and lower arms as you coordinate the rotating movement of your wrists, arms, and body. The plane in which your arms move also influences the moment of impact: The angle of approach will be steep if the plane is steep and vice versa.

Lie Too Flat or Too Steep at Impact

In general, if the end of the club handle is too low at impact, the club was also too low at the address position, meaning that the tip of the club was off the ground, pointing into the air. The reason could be that the club is too long or that you chose the wrong club for a lie that was too upright.

The end of the handle is too high because you hit too early or too late, so that you have dissolved the angle between the arm and the club too early or too late. Furthermore, the horizontal angle of impact also influences the position of the shaft at the moment of impact. If the club approaches the ball from the outside or

the inside, the possibility is much greater that the end of the club handle was too high.

Flight of the Ball

In the following section, I will try to familiarize you with the complex law that governs the flight path of a ball.

You will hear me talk about the direction a ball takes when starting out on its flight. Since that depends to a great degree on the approach, when I talk about "starting" direction, I mean the direction the player assumes during the approach.

A struck ball can move in three different directions: to the left, to the right, and straight ahead.

When the ball is in the air, it can fly straight ahead, veer off to the left, or veer off to the right. The illustrations show all kinds of possibilities that result from clubs of different lengths.

The best way to analyze the flight of a ball is with a club that has little loft (wood or iron). When using short clubs with a great deal of loft, a ball produces so much backspin that any possible sidespin will not come into play. For example, a ball hit with a 9 iron rarely assumes a strong curve in the air.

If you want to make corrections on your own, you must know the laws that govern the flight of a ball, since the ball is all that you can see.

To understand how the individual factors at play at the moment of impact influence the flight path of a particular ball, assume that you hit the ball at the sweet spot and that at the moment of impact the shaft had the proper angle to the ground, based on its lie. In practical terms, of course, such simplification is not realistic, because a ball might start out to the right simply because it was hit with the heel or the tip or because the end of the handle was too high.

A ball will always have a sidespin when, at the moment of impact, the clubface is not at right angles to the direction of the swing. The initial direction of the ball depends on the direction of the swing and the position of the clubface at impact. As the speed of the clubhead decreases, the position of the clubface becomes much more important. In putting, for instance, the direction the ball will start out in is primarily determined by the position of the putter. The often-stated fact that the direction the ball takes always depends on the movements of the club is false. You can easily confirm this by taking a few practice shots. Rotate the clubface firmly in one direction while trying to drive the ball for distance. You will find that the ball always starts out in a direction that is somewhere between these two extremes.

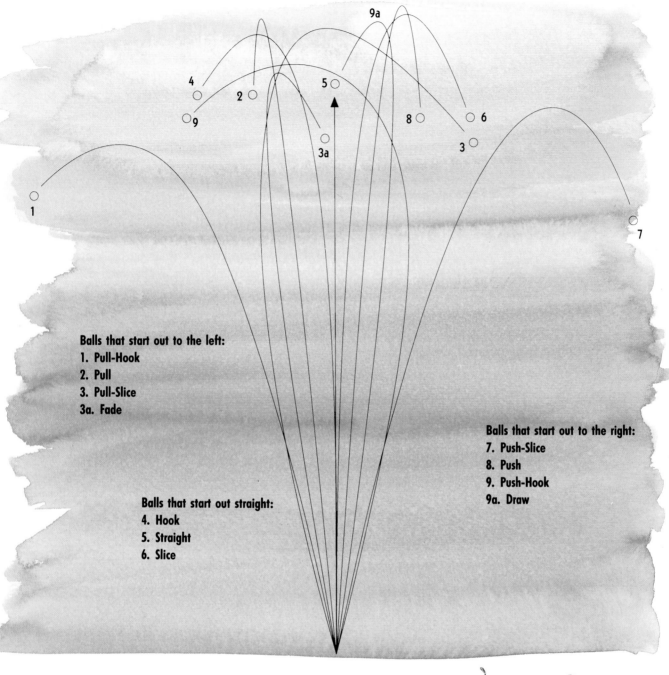

Balls that start out to the left:
1. Pull-Hook
2. Pull
3. Pull-Slice
3a. Fade

Balls that start out to the right:
7. Push-Slice
8. Push
9. Push-Hook
9a. Draw

Balls that start out straight:
4. Hook
5. Straight
6. Slice

The speed of the club-head depends on the energy created and converted during the backswing.

A discussion of every possible way of hitting a ball will help you to identify specific ball-in-flight problems. (The numbers refer to the drawing on page 81.)

Let's start with the **straight** shot, the shot that travels to the target in a straight line (5). Here, the club moves at a right angle to the target at the moment of impact, the clubhead moves inside-to-in, and the position of the clubface is vertical to the intended line to the target.

During the **pull** movement (2), the club-head crosses the intended line to the target from the outside in, and the clubface is vertical to the path of the swing. With a short iron, you can pull the ball if the clubface tilts to the extreme left. This has more influence on the initial direction of the ball than it would with a longer club because of the limited speed of the club-head. Often the ball will not veer farther to the left because a short iron gives a ball considerably more backspin. The sidespin is, obviously, less of a factor.

During the **push** movement (8), the clubhead crosses the intended line to the target from the inside out, and the club-face is vertical to the path of the swing at the time of impact. Here, too, the ball can start out moving to the right because the clubface tilted to the right at impact. With a longer club, the ball might have veered farther to the right, so that one can say that the path of the swing was from the inside out and that the clubface was vertical to the path of the swing.

With the **pull-hook** movement (1), it is impossible to determine the path of the swing by looking only at the flight path of

Bernhard Langer during an approach shot. In order to give the ball sufficient backspin, the club must move through the ball in a downward motion.

the ball. Nevertheless, the clubface angled to the left in relation to the path of the swing. You can't determine the precise path of the swing since the ball started out moving to the left simply because of the extreme angle of the clubface. The swing didn't necessarily have to move from the outside in. To pinpoint the sequence of movements precisely, examine the divot, look at the video, or analyze your other shots.

What is true for the pull-hook is true of the **push-slice** (7), except that you angle the clubface to the extreme right. The **pull-slice** (3) and the **fade** (3a) occur when the club moves from the outside in and the clubface is at a right angle to the path of swing, more so in the case of the pull-slice and less so in the case of the fade.

The same holds true for the **push-hook** (9) and the **draw** (9a). Here, the club moves from the inside out, and the clubface is at a left angle to the path of the club, less in the case of the draw and more in the case of the push-hook.

Even if the ball starts out in the direction of the intended line to the target, a **slice** (6) occurs when the club moves through the ball from inside out. In relation to the path of the swing, the clubhead tilts to the right, since the ball would start out moving to the right if the path of the swing moved correctly from the inside in. We may conclude that the club moves on a path from the outside in, if the ball starts out straight.

The **hook** (4) is the mirror image of the slice. The swing moves from the inside out, and the clubface tilts to the left.

A perfect divot starts immediately after the ball and points slightly to the left of the target. The depth of the divot should be uniform.

Divot

A few words about the divot helps in analyzing the situation at impact. When using an iron, a perfect divot should start immediately after the ball because the club at impact is in a down movement. The divot points slightly to the left of the target because after impact the club is already moving to the inside. The divot should also be uniformly deep because at impact the club is parallel to the ground.

If the divot points to the extreme right or left, you can assume that the club was moving through the ball from the inside out or from the outside in. If the divot starts in front of the ball, the deepest point of the swing was too far to the right, caused by a spoonlike movement or by a club that moves through the ball from the inside out (see also page 80).

If your divots are too deep, the plane of your arm or the angle at impact is too steep. The cause of either can be the club moving through the ball from the outside in. If your center of gravity at impact shifts too far to the left, you'll get the same result.

When there are no divots, the plane of your arm was too flat. Divots that are deeper on the outside indicate that at the moment of impact the shaft of the club was not in the position required for its lie because the end of the club handle was too high.

Most Common Mistakes

This chapter, as far as a ball in flight is concerned, will help you deal with problems involving the flight of the ball. The following paragraphs list deviations from the ideal at the moment of impact and explain the mistakes responsible for them. We discussed the reasons for the mistakes in the previous chapter.

Slice

A slice is the result of a clubface that (in relation to the path of the clubhead) tilts to the right of the intended line to the target. By slice, I mean all shots where the ball veers to the right, regardless of its initial direction.

Often a clubface opens when the club approaches the ball from the outside.

Topping might occur when the clubhead, at the lowest point (when viewed from the front), is too far to the left of the ball.

Topping might also occur when the clubhead, at the lowest point of the swing path, is above the center of the ball.

But more than anything else, the position of the clubface is responsible for a slice. In many cases, the curve of the swing from outside-to-in is only a reaction to a ball that is veering off to the right. Very rarely, the heel of the club being too far in the air causes a slice.

Hook

A hook is the result of a clubface that (in relation to the path of the swing) tilts to the left (closed). As in the case of a slice, the tilt might be caused by an incorrect swing curve, but here, the club moves through the ball too much from inside-to-out.

Topping

Topping, hitting the ball above its center, occurs most frequently to beginners. It is particularly frustrating because the ball does not become airborne. A player can top the ball in three different ways:

1. At its lowest point in the arc, the clubhead is too high, making it impossible to reach the ball at or below the center.
2. At its lowest point, the clubhead is to the right of the ball, and the club is already in an upward movement when it hits the ball.
3. At its lowest point, the clubhead is too far to the left of the ball, so that, at impact, the clubhead is too high for a proper hit.

In the past we thought that only the first of these three possibilities was responsible for topping the ball. However, it is actually the least common reason.

Topping is, assuredly, not the result of taking your eyes off the ball before impact to see where the ball is heading. After seven years of teaching, using video cameras, high-speed shutters that produce sharp images even at high speeds, and time-lapse photography, I am still waiting for the first golfer who takes his eyes off the ball before impact to look at the target.

Flexing the left arm is also never the reason for topping a ball. Straightening the body during the impact phase, frequently thought of as a possible reason, occurs only when the clubhead digs too deeply into the ground.

The real reasons for the first possibility, topping because the clubhead is too high, are:

1. During the backswing, if the hands are not high enough in the air (flat arm plane), they will not come back close enough to the body. Instead, they will move forward.
2. The club does not swing low enough to the ground if you hold the shaft too horizontally. The club always has the tendency to swing in the direction that the shaft is pointing. So, the shaft should always point in the direction of the intended line of flight. In this case, the shaft points above the ball, and (assuming that the player doesn't do any manipulation) the clubface will hit the ball above the center.
3. If the shoulders move on a plane that is too flat (left shoulder is too high), the player "grows taller," and, in order to hit the ball, he must "grow smaller." In addition, a flat shoulder plane usually leads to a flat arm plane, one of the main reasons for topping.

Reasons for the second possibility, the clubhead at the lowest point being to the right of the ball, are:

1. The path of the swing was from inside-to-out and the club hit the ground before hitting the ball or passed over the ground but hit the ball during the upward movement. This problem also causes many balls to start out moving to the right. The divots are to the right of the ball and point to the right.
2. Even though the swing pointed in the direction of the target, the deepest part of the swing was to the ball's right, making the angle at impact too flat.

Topping might occur when the clubhead, at the lowest point of the swing (from the player's point of view), is to the right of the ball.

The reasons for the clubhead being too far to the left or behind the ball at the lowest point of the swing are:

1. The club is hitting through the ball outside-to-in. The club doesn't reach the ball at the lowest point of the swing, and the clubhead is too high for hitting the ball correctly.

   The reason for this type of topping is that other hits start out moving to the left, or they slice. Should there be a divot, it usually points to the left.

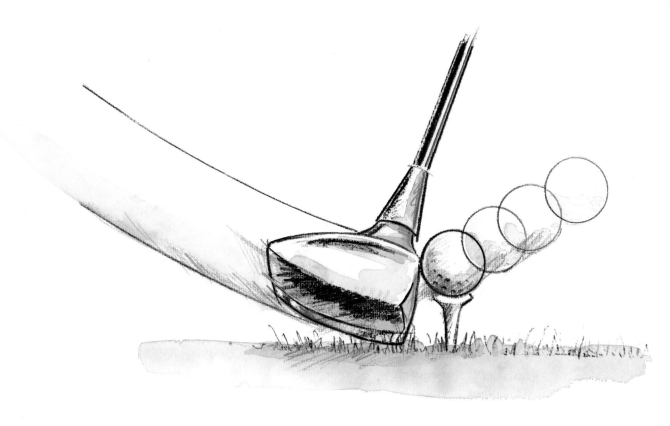

Sometimes the club hits so far above that the ball leaves an indentation in the ground.

2. The angle between your arm and the club dissolved too late. If there is still an angle between your arm and the club at impact, you can't establish the original radius (of the arm and club) again, and you hit the ball too far above the center.

The golfer who has a tendency towards this kind of topping should try to speed up his downswing by dissolving the angle at the wrist joint early. This should give him the feeling that he will hit the ground before hitting the ball.

Fat Hits

Fat hits are shots in which the club hits the ground too early (too far to the right). Players almost always view them incor-

In most cases, skying occurs when the vertical angle at impact is too steep.

rectly. Immediately after such a shot, a player thinks that the next time he should avoid hitting the ground, because a divot is proof that the shot was bad. In reality, all he has to do is to hit the ground farther to the left. A divot is not negative; in fact, it is absolutely essential for irons.

In order to figure out the reason for a fat shot, you must examine the divot closely. If the divot points to the right of the target, you know that the swing curve moved inside-to-out. This is the reason the club hit the ground too early. If, on the other hand, the divot points straight at the target, or even to the left of it, the angle at impact was too flat (see page 68 for details).

Skying

Skying the ball with a wood seldom occurs because the tee was too high. Actually, it is usually the club that approaches the ball too steeply. The upper edge of the clubhead hits the ball, sending it up in the air rather than forward (see also page 78).

Pull

Pulling occurs when the clubface (in relation to the intended line to the target) tilts to the right, and when the club hits through the ball outside-to-in. In order to determine the cause, check your swing when you don't pull the ball.

If you usually slice the ball, correct the path of the swing from the outside to the inside. If you usually hook the ball, correct the left tilt of the clubface.

Push

A push occurs when the clubface (in relation to the intended line of flight) tilts to the right, and when the clubhead swings through the ball inside-to-out. To determine which is the cause, analyze shots when you don't push the ball. Correct the path of the swing if you don't pull the ball; correct the position of the clubface if you don't slice other balls.

Socket or Shank

The name for this hitting mistake comes from the part of the club that hits the ball. When using an iron, a ball hit with the socket starts out moving to the extreme right; when using a wood, to the extreme left.

As previously mentioned, you can hit the ball two ways with the socket. If, during the backswing, the club and/or your arms swing on a plane that is too flat, the clubhead will move too far out and hit the ball with the heel. If that is the case, check the position and direction of the ball. On the other hand, if the ball is too far to the left, your right shoulder is too far forward during the address and, therefore, points too far to the left. In such

A socket, or shank, is a dreaded mistake usually caused by a flat backswing or a delayed hit.

an address position, the club would normally swing far outside the intended line of flight.

In general, a player notices this subconsciously and swings the club more to the inside. As far as the target is concerned, this might be the correct way of swinging the club down. However, from the player's point of view, the swing is too far to the inside. This mistake usually happens during short shots. A player might have heard that these shots should be open (oriented to the left). There is nothing wrong with that, if you keep in mind that only your feet should point to the left. In most cases, though, players include their shoulders in this correction. Even if a full swing moves on a flat plane during the beginning of the backswing, it is possible to pull back the club during the second phase of the backswing. This returns it to the correct plane. In the case of a half swing, this compensating movement is very difficult to make.

Delaying the hit when dissolving the angle between your lower arm and the club causes the clubface to rotate too far to the right at impact, resulting in a shank, or socket. With a rotated clubface, the heel of the club is closer to the ball than the tip, also leading to a shank. With a full swing, you usually slice the ball. If this is your problem, check your grip and, if necessary, turn your hands farther to the right. During the downswing, make sure that the clubhead catches up with your hands at the right time and does not hang back at impact. With the proper corrections, slicing long drives and hitting the ball with the heel of the club should be things of the past.

It is rare that a shank and a hook happen together. Sockets occur because the club is hitting through the ball inside-to-out.

Hitting with the Tip

As is the case with the shank, either of two mistakes can cause hitting with the tip of the club: The club plane and/or the arm plane is too steep, or at impact the club-face tilts to the left. It's easy to see the results of the mistakes when watching a ball in flight. If the ball veers to the right, the plane of the club or the arm was too steep. If the ball veers to the left, the clubface tilted to the left. If the former is the case, check your address position. If, at the beginning of the swing, the upper body leans too far forward, the shoulders will dip down during the downswing,

usually leading to a steep arm plane. To correct this mistake, practise on a slope or use a high tee. This forces you to swing your arms and club farther back. During the downswing, the club will move farther out, hitting the ball in the center of the clubhead.

Because of a more rounded swing, the club will be more open during the back-swing, and your arms will be more closed. The balls you hit won't veer off to the right anymore.

If you hit balls with the tip, and they veer to the left, check your grip. If necessary, rotate your hands farther to the left. If this does not eliminate the problem, pay attention during the downswing and make sure that you don't engage only your arms and your hands. Your hips also need to rotate out of the way. This prevents the club from moving out ahead of your hands, causing the clubface to close too early.

During the backswing, the lower part of your body should not move either to the right ...

Insufficient Distance

To drive a golf ball for distance, you have to hit the ball at the optimal moment of impact, and all six factors that influence the moment of impact must be in place. The idea that the speed of the clubhead is the cause of a short drive is only correct when all the other factors are perfect. Most of the time, the ball has not travelled far enough because the clubface tilted, the ball missed the sweet spot, or the club hit through the ball from inside-to-in. However, if you are sure that all the correct factors are in place and your ball still does not travel far enough, read page 72 again to find the reasons why the speed of your clubhead is too slow.

Inconsistency

Many golf players are inconsistent, but are not simply making new mistakes at every turn. As we discussed in the previous pages, one mistake can have many different consequences. Therefore, golfers should first try to see if there is a pattern to their mistakes. In most cases, there is only a single reason for them.

In addition, poor body posture and mistakes in the flow of movements are often the reason a ball misbehaves. But these are mistakes we have discussed previously, for instance, moving the lower half of the body. If, during the backswing, the right leg and the upper body shift to the right, the weight rests on the outside

of the right foot and doesn't create enough tension between the upper and lower body. The lower body, particularly the right leg, should not shift to the right. It should support the rotation of the upper body. A good way of dealing with this problem is to push the tip of an umbrella into the ground next to your right leg while you are in the address position. This makes it easy to rotate the upper body during the backswing without moving the right leg.

As we discussed in the chapter on the swing, in the original position the body should rotate around the spine. This is difficult for the beginner, since during the backswing, the club and the arms move

. . . or to the left (left). **It should provide support for the upper body. To practise, you might want to push the tip of an umbrella into the ground next to your right leg** (right).

89

upwards, but the body should not. To practise, stand in front of a large mirror where you can observe your movements and correct possible mistakes. The feeling you develop during practice swings transfers to the actual swing when you hit the ball on the golf course. Don't try to avoid the tension that develops in your right leg and back.

When players are not economical with their efforts when attempting a shot, they usually have very little to show for it. Consciously or unconsciously, some players try to compensate with an exaggerated backswing. Although this does work sometimes, it never works consistently. If you are not getting sufficient distance, try to concentrate on hitting the ball correctly instead of increasing your backswing. In addition, remember that your backswing is actually much longer than you think it is.

At the end of your swing, make sure that your grip has not loosened, that your arms have not moved too far away from your body, and that the original distance between your hands and chest has not changed. If the latter should occur, concentrate on pushing your right arm away from you rather than trying to stretch your left arm, which usually leads to unintended muscle tension.

Another mistake that occurs when a player swings a golf club is a reverse pivot.

In this case, the player shifts his weight to the left during the backswing and to the right during the downswing—in other words, the wrong way. This usually happens when a player tries to keep his head in one position without paying attention to the lateral rotation.

If this is your problem, throw a golf ball and watch how your weight automatically shifts to the right when you reach back and how it moves to the left during the forward movement. Of course, the lateral movement that occurs when you swing a golf club is not quite as pronounced as when you throw a ball, but the principle is the same.

The reverse pivot is another mistake. During the backswing, the weight shifts to the left (right)**, and during the downswing, it shifts to the right** (opposite page) **...**

... perhaps because the player tries to keep the head in a fixed position. During a proper swing, the head moves around the spine with the body's rotation—to the right during the backswing and to the left during the downswing.

MISTAKES AND THEIR CORRECTION

- Only the factors at the moment of impact determine the direction of the ball in flight: hitting the sweet spot, the speed of the clubhead, the position of the clubface, the horizontal angle at impact, the vertical angle at impact, and the club's lie at impact.
- Any deviations from the optimal situation at impact result from mistakes made in the swing.
- You can analyze the situation at the moment of impact by examining the flight path of the ball (at the start and if it veers off), the divot, and the way the handle of the club rotates in your hands.
- You are making one or more mistakes if the flight path of your balls differs from one shot to the next.
- Golfers usually make the same mistakes over and over again.

THE REASONS FOR THE MOST COMMON MISTAKES

SLICE

- Grip: hands rotate too far to the left
- Stance: ball too far to the left
- Posture: shoulders point to the left
- Left wrist: dorsal flexion
- Downswing: late hit with too much body rotation
- Arm plane: too steep
- Club hits the ball from the outside

LOW HIT AT THE TEE

- Club moves through the ball outside-to-in
- Center of body's gravity too far in front of the ball
- Arm plane too steep

HOOK

- Grip: hands rotate too far to the right
- Stance: ball too far to the right
- Posture: shoulders point to the right
- Left wrist: volar flexion
- Downswing: early hit with insufficient hip rotation
- Clubhead too far forward on impact

FAT HIT

- Club moves through the ball inside-to-out
- Hitting too early
- Center of body's gravity too far behind the ball
- Shoulders dipping

HITTING WITH THE TIP

- Plane of arm and/or club too steep
- Clubface closed because of insufficient body rotation during downswing
- Club moves through the ball either extremely inside-to-out or outside-to-in

TOPPING

- Plane of arms, shoulders, or club too flat
- Club moves through the ball inside-to-out
- Club moves upwards before impact (early hit)
- Club moves through the ball outside-to-in
- Delayed hit

INSUFFICIENT DISTANCE

- Insufficient flexion of the wrists during backswing
- Insufficient rotation of the shoulder or too much rotation of the lower body during backswing
- Ball hit poorly (sweet spot, angle at impact, position of clubface at impact)

SHANK

- Plane of arm and/or club too flat
- Clubface open (usually late hit)
- Club moving through the ball either extremely inside-to-out or outside-to-in

Britain still owns the Royal Cape Golf Club, founded in 1885. This spectacular course, with its view of Tafelberg, was often the site of the South African Championships.

The SHORT GAME

The short game involves distances up to 45 yards (41 m). Although the short game makes up about 60 percent of the game, most players only spend about 10 percent of their practice on it.

Either golfers feel that short drives are boring, or they would rather impress their companions with long drives. Of course, there's nothing wrong with that attitude if your score at the end of the game is less important than other people's opinion.

Most players insist that having fun is the reason they play golf. They use this feeling to rationalize not paying enough attention to their short game. However, I ask myself if those who occasionally shine with brilliant long drives are really all that satisfied when they watch their companions finish first because they did not give away as many shots.

I will try to explain why I think that a good short game is much more satisfying than good long drives. Imagine that you play a par 5 hole twice. The first time, you hit a perfectly straight 275-yard (250-m)

Compared to American golf courses, where high approach shots are necessary because of the design of the course (many bunkers, high grass, and water traps), approach shots on golf courses in England must be played much lower due to the hard greens and high winds.

drive, followed by a 250-yard (230-m) shot with a 3 wood right onto the green. However, even though you have a chance for an eagle, you leave the green with par (five shots).

Now play the same hole again. This time, you slice the ball with a 5 wood into the rough. The ball only covers a distance of 175 yards (160 m). From the right rough, you hook the ball with a 5 iron 140 yards (130 m) into the left rough. The next shot, using the 5 iron, is a fat hit that only goes 100 yards (90 m) into the next fairway bunker. With a 7 iron, you barely manage to get the ball onto the green. However, you are able to hit the hole from 22 yards (20 m) away, leaving the green with the same five shots. Which of the two scenarios would give you more satisfaction? The second, of course. After the

first, you will stand at the tee of the next hole hopping mad, taking even more chances. After the second, you are very excited that you were able to leave with par. You start the next hole feeling that you were able to play par even though the long drives turned out rather poorly, and now you continue your game much more relaxed.

Here's a list of reasons why a golfer should put more emphasis on the short game:

• Practising short shots pays off faster than practising long drives. Many times golfers have to admit that their game is worse after practising long drives! This is less likely to happen after a practice round of putting. In addition, when golfers practise putting properly, most of them improve the quality of their game considerably without having to change their technique. It takes much more time to see a similar improvement in long drives.

• Even if a player's putting technique is all wrong, correcting it can be done quickly. However, it might take years to correct the technique of long drives!

• For drives under 45 yards (41 m), a player's age isn't that important because the technique does not rely on flexibility, speed, or power.

• In the short game, a player's form is more consistent than it is in long drives.

Since the number of possible situations around the green is almost limitless, I will restrict myself to the basic techniques. You will use these in most cases, even when some changes have to be made in the grip or when a ball is in a poor lie.

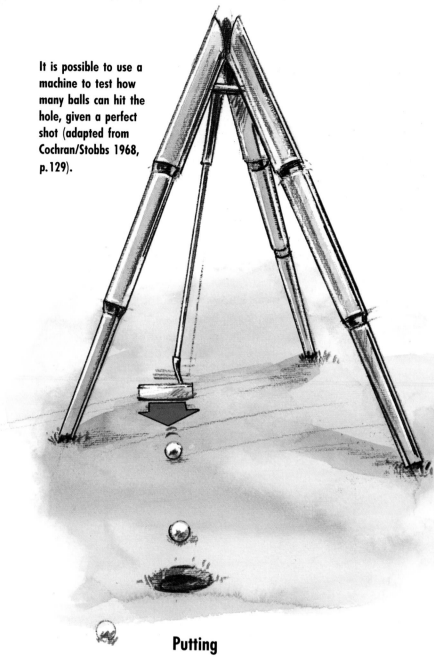

It is possible to use a machine to test how many balls can hit the hole, given a perfect shot (adapted from Cochran/Stobbs 1968, p.129).

Putting

The putter is the most frequently used club in golf. Forty-three percent of all shots are putts. Golfers who have difficulty putting will never be able to play their best. This chapter will help you to raise your putting skill to a level that you never believed possible.

Science of the Green

For years, people thought that putting was an art that a golfer either did or did not possess. Top professionals still seem to use such different techniques with such great success (you would be hard put to find two pros with the same technique) that no correlation seems to exist between technique and success. Many who practise putting without success tend to agree with that theory.

By now we know why so many believe this. Unlike hitting long drives, hitting the ball with a putter does not give the player reliable feedback. Because balls might not be perfectly round and might have pitch and spike marks and because the green might have foot imprints and protruding holes (see page 100), a ball seldom rolls in the direction it would under perfect circumstances. Thus, you can do everything right and still end up far away from the hole. The opposite is also true. You can make mistakes when hitting the ball and still land in the hole.

If you make a putt that is not ideal, you are often unable to say what went wrong by watching the behavior of the ball. For instance, the reason the ball rolls past the hole on the left side could be an imperfection in the ball or the green, or other factors at impact, such as the clubface being tilted to the left, the club hitting through the ball inside-to-out, or the heel of the clubhead hitting the ball. In any case, you would only know that the ball rolled past the hole on the left side.

To see how successful a player can be at putting, experts conducted the following test on a very good green: A machine released a large number of balls towards a hole from about 12 feet (3.5 m) away, always at the same speed and in the exact direction of the hole. The success rate was only 50 percent. This means that a player, even if putting perfectly every time from this distance, will still miss the hole every second try.

What then, you might ask, is a very good player's percentage from this distance? Statisticians from the PGA tour have examined this very closely. According to their figures, under tournament conditions, the average pro will hole a ball 20 percent of the time. In most cases, it is impossible to decide if the success or failure was due to the player.

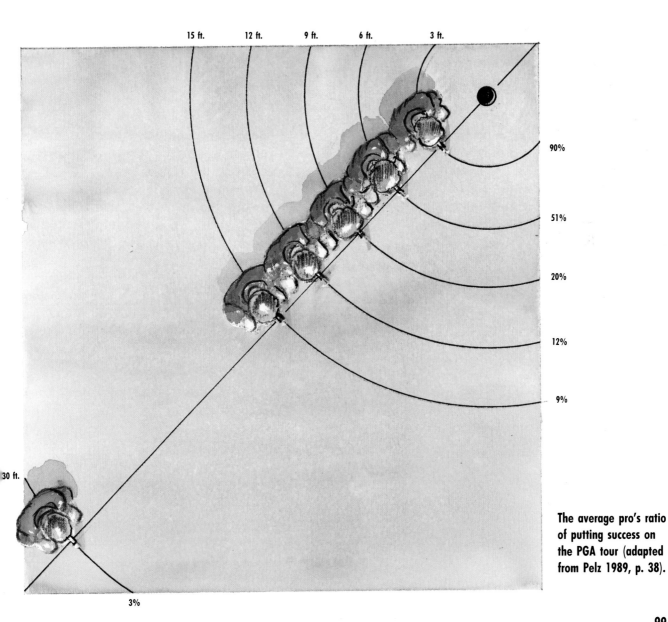

The average pro's ratio of putting success on the PGA tour (adapted from Pelz 1989, p. 38).

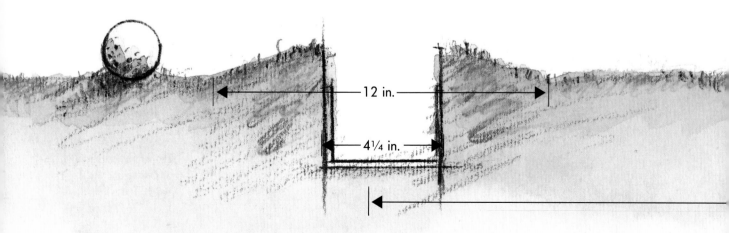

How can it be that a ball lined up and putted with perfect speed in the direction of the hole has only a 50-percent chance of actually falling in the hole?

First of all, in golf we are not dealing with perfectly round balls. To prove this, put a golf ball in a glass of saltwater. Be sure the solution is strong enough for the ball to float. After the ball comes to rest, mark the central point of the exposed part of the ball with a waterproof pen. Put the ball back in the water. If a different part of the ball is above the surface of the water, the center of gravity of the ball is truly in the center. In most cases, however, the same part of the ball will be above the surface. This proves that the center of gravity is not in the center, but rather below the center, immediately under the mark. Of course, such an "egg" won't roll in a straight line and can roll past a hole without any outside influence.

You can determine the quality of a ball by the time it takes to come to rest. The longer it takes, the more perfect the ball.

How can you use this information?
- You might want to separate out those balls that are a lot less than perfect and use them only for practice sessions.
- When putting, position the ball so that the marked point is on top. The ball will then move vertically and not away from the intended direction.

Other reasons for a low percentage of holed balls are impressions in the ground made by shoes, spikes, and pitches. Even if you can barely detect it, a tiny imprint is like a deep pit for the ball. Some pit marks equal 15 percent of the diameter of the ball. Greens are never as smooth as a billiard table, and this is the reason why you can't putt with one-hundred-percent accuracy.

However, footprints are the main reason why so many balls that should get into the hole don't. A group of four golfers leaves about five hundred footprints behind, from reading the putting line, marking their balls, moving the flag, and putting. Although those footprints are more concentrated directly around the

Each hole practically turns into a crater. While nobody steps on the immediate space surrounding a hole, a 6-foot (2-m) area around it sees lots of heavy traffic (adapted from Pelz 1989, p. 35).

12 in.

4¼ in.

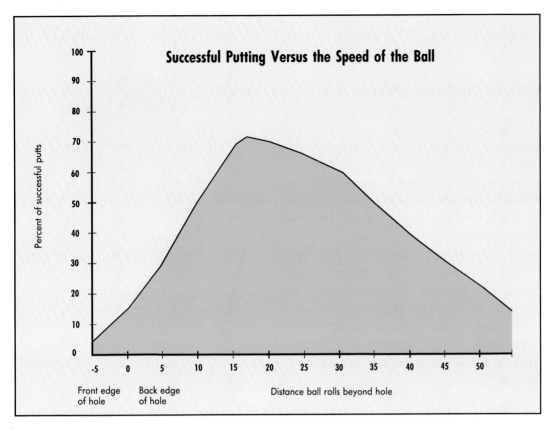

Successful Putting Versus the Speed of the Ball

Percent of successful putts

Front edge of hole

Back edge of hole

Distance ball rolls beyond hole

This table shows how the possibility of a ball falling into the hole changes, depending on its speed. The greatest chance for hitting the hole occurs when the ball travels at a speed that would allow it to roll 17 inches (43 cm) beyond the hole (adapted from Pelz 1989, p. 128).

hole, nobody steps in the immediate vicinity of the hole, so that the soil around it is not pressed down. Since the 6-foot (2-m) surrounding area gets so much use, the soil in the less "travelled" areas expands upwards, turning each hole into a reverse crater. This considerably increases the ratio of missed balls to holed balls. What can be done about it?

- During practice sessions, play as early as possible because fewer golfers on the green will have compressed the soil.
- The ball must have a certain speed as it reaches the hole. The slower the speed, the more likely it is that the green will deflect the ball from its intended course. But the speed should not be too high, or the ball will hop over the hole.

6 ft.

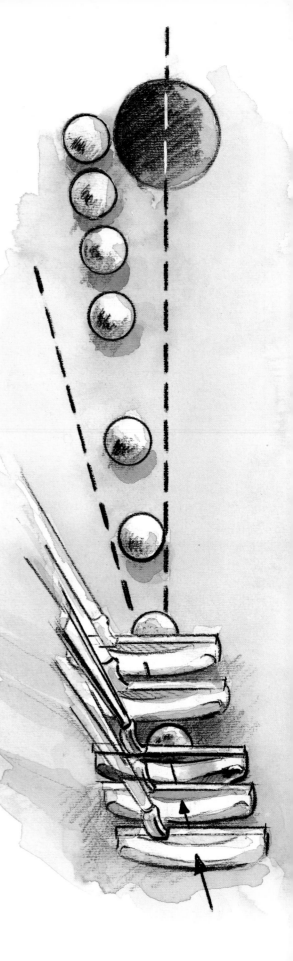

Factors at the Moment of Impact

You probably expect to find instructions on the correct grip, good posture and position, and correct movements at the beginning of a chapter on putting. However, you will find these at the end because the ball cares very little how you hold the putter as long as you are relaxed, and you think positive.

Of course, there are grips, postures, and movements that are more or less suited for putting. But first, I want to make clear to you what is responsible for whether or not the ball reaches the proper speed and rolls in the proper direction.

A good putt depends primarily on three factors:

1. At impact, the clubhead is moving in the direction in which the ball should roll.
2. At impact, the clubhead is at right angles to the direction the ball should roll.
3. The clubhead must hit the ball squarely with the sweet spot.

Unfortunately, a player can only see the first factor. You cannot see with the naked eye if the clubface is straight or if you hit the ball with the sweet spot. But the first factor is only partially responsible, because if you miss the right direction by 10 percent, the ball will start off in the wrong direction by only 2 degrees. However, if the clubface points 10 percent farther to the right at impact, the ball starts out 8 degrees farther to the right and will not veer to the right. It will only start out that way, and, because of the sidespin, it will roll a shorter distance. If the putter does not make contact on the sweet spot, assuming that you gave it the right energy, the ball will never go into the hole. The shot will be much too short. Because of the rotation, the ball loses its momentum.

If the angle of the putter is off by 20 percent, the ball will start out only 4 degrees in the wrong direction, provided that all other factors were right at impact (adapted from Pelz 1989, p. 50).

It's difficult to determine precisely how much this factor influences the result since the distance the ball falls short of the hole depends on the kind of putter used and how far you miss the sweet spot. If you have to choose which of the three factors to master perfectly, choose the third. Here at least, you have a chance, and you will seldom need more than three tries. Three putts are usually necessary when the ball stops short or goes far beyond the hole on the first try, and not because it went too far to the right or to the left. In addition, the first two factors usually offset each another.

But now let's take a closer look at each of those three fundamental factors involved at impact mentioned earlier.

The putting path may run directly along the intended line to the hole, veer off to the left, or veer to the right. However, a great amount of uncertainty exists over which direction the putter head should be moving in before and after impact. We realize that with a full swing an inside-to-in movement is not possible when a club swings in a circle. The conclusion most frequently drawn is that, basically, the same holds true for putting. However, the proper path of the clubhead is not circular for two reasons:

1. When putting, the shoulders do not rotate. They move in a pendulumlike, dipping motion.
2. The hands are in the correct position (when viewed from the front) exactly below the shoulders.

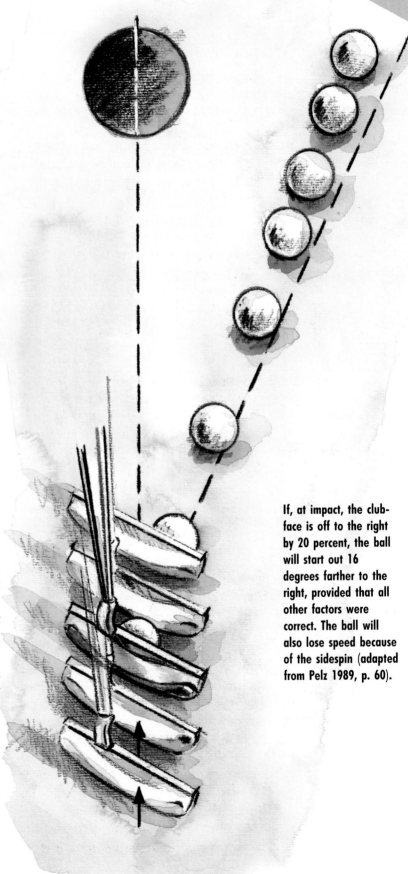

If, at impact, the club-face is off to the right by 20 percent, the ball will start out 16 degrees farther to the right, provided that all other factors were correct. The ball will also lose speed because of the sidespin (adapted from Pelz 1989, p. 60).

The lower end of the pendulum of a clock (swinging perpendicular to the ground) always moves in a straight line (when viewed from above). The lower end of the pendulum only moves in a circle if the clock is tilting. In putting, this corresponds to a situation in which the hands of the player are not below his shoulders. In an ideal situation, this means that if the clubhead is above the intended

width of the putter head plus ¾ inch (2 cm) apart. Position your putter between the two pieces and hit a few balls. If all the shots are "silent," the position of your putter is correct. If the ball hits either one of the pieces, the path of the club was wrong. For this exercise, the ball should not move more than approximately 18 feet (5 m) and no actual hole should be included. If you reach a success rate of

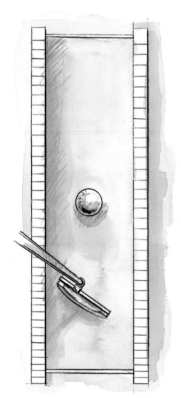
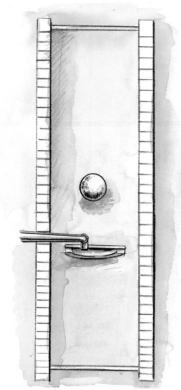
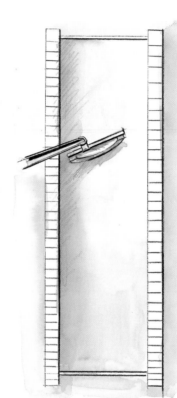

The putter must not rotate during the swing. In most cases, you open the club during the backswing and close it again when hitting through the ball. For a putter that is moving in a straight path, this is wrong and diminishes the chances for the clubface to be vertical to the intended line to the target at impact (adapted from Pelz 1989, p. 63).

line to the target, the clubface will always be perpendicular to it. Because of the club's circular path, the clubface must always be open and relatively close to the intended line to the target. But this is not the case when putting. When you hit the ball is not that important as long as the putter remains above the intended line at all times. The question of the position of the ball becomes relative. In order to test this theory or when you practise, lay down two pieces of wood. Place them the

over 80 percent (meaning 80 percent of your balls are silent), move the pieces of wood closer together. In addition, mark the pieces with lines perpendicular to the intended line to the target. This allows you to check to see if the clubface is still parallel to the lines.

Even though the position of the clubface at impact is more important than the path of the putter, most golfers never spend much time practising it because they don't know how!

Tom Kite, one of the world's best putters, demonstrates the "left-hand-below" grip.

To check the putter's path, use two pieces of wood, or, as seen here, a putter track.

In order to determine if the clubface tilts at impact, putt two balls at the same time. The sweet spot must be exactly behind the point where the two balls touch each other, and the distance of the putter to both balls must be equal.

To find out if you are a hooker or a slicer (whether the clubface tilts to the right or to the left at impact), try the following test: Put two balls next to each other in front of your putter. The putter should be equidistant from both balls. Hit both balls a distance of about 18 feet (5 m). If the putter is exactly perpendicular to the intended line to the target, the putter will hit both balls simultaneously, and both balls will roll next to each other at the same speed. If the club tilts to the left at impact, the ball on the outside will be hit first, moving ahead of the other ball and rolling farther than the one on the inside. If the club tilts to the right at impact, the ball on the inside will be hit first, moving ahead of the other ball and rolling farther than the one on the outside. It is easy to determine how much the putter tilts by determining how far apart the balls are. This test should become part of your putting-practice routine.

Hitting the ball with the sweet spot is a prerequisite for successful putting. First, find out where the sweet spot is on your club. Suspend the putter between two fingers on an angle (the same way the putter leans when putting). Use a tee to tap along the clubface. The sweet spot is the spot where you can push backwards without the club twisting or rotating.

In order to determine which part of the clubface hits the ball, place one ball ¼ inch (½ cm) in front of the tip and another one ¼ inch (½ cm) behind the heel of the putter. Remove the putter and place a third ball in front of the sweet spot so that all three balls are lined up in a row. Try to putt the middle ball, without aiming at a hole, a distance of 18 feet (5 m). If you hit the ball with the sweet spot, the balls on the outside won't be touched. On the other hand, if you hit the ball with the heel, you'll also hit the ball positioned at the tip. This will give you immediate feedback. The same holds true when you hit the ball with the tip of the putter. Use your normal putting technique; don't try to make corrections according to the result. In most cases, you will detect that you have a definite tendency to hit in one direction. It is very unusual for a player to hit a ball with the heel sometimes and at other times with the tip. This test, too, should become part of your practice routine as soon as you have determined what your tendency is and have made the proper improvements to your technique.

To avoid the cumbersome placement of the three balls, you can also use special training aids. One such sweet-spot training aid attaches to the putter. A ball that is hit with the sweet spot will roll straight ahead. On the other hand, a ball hit with the heel will veer off to the right, and a ball hit with the tip will roll to the left.

The sweet spot is the spot where you can push the putter with a tee without causing the putter to twist or rotate.

In order to find out if a ball is hit with the sweet spot, line up three balls and putt the one in the middle.

Before going on to the next chapter, determine your putter's path during the swing. Are you rotating the putter during the backswing or when hitting through the ball? Are you rotating the club on impact, and if so, in what direction? Are you missing the sweet spot?

If a ball is hit with the tip or the heel of a putter with a training aid attached, it will veer off to the left or to the right.

Use a special training aid if you want to save yourself the trouble of lining up three balls.

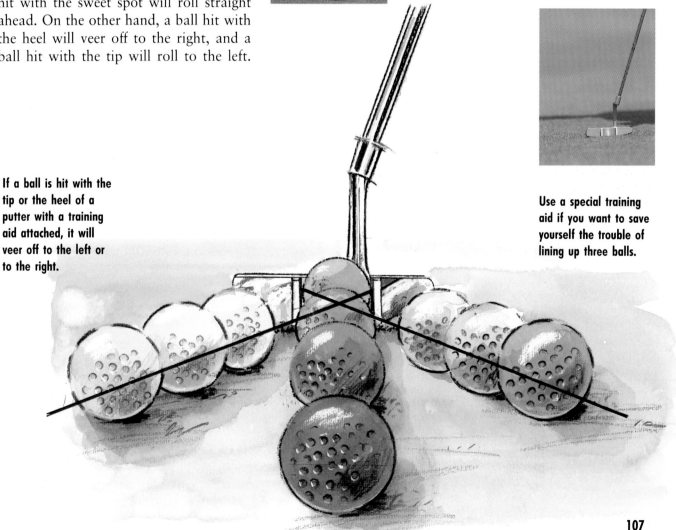

Technique

Don't expect your success rate to improve by leaps and bounds just because you begin to use the techniques discussed in this chapter. Marked improvement is mainly a question of how much you practise. As a teacher, I have noticed that certain problems simply can't be overcome as long as basic techniques are incorrect. After a period of adjustment and practice, players very quickly reach their previous level of putting success and increase their level of expertise over time.

When putting, the wrists should remain totally passive since the ball only rolls a short distance but must be accurate. (When hitting long drives, the flexion of the hands provides speed to the clubhead.) To accomplish this, use a grip in which the left hand is below the right hand and all fingers touch the handle. Since the hands are more lateral on the putter handle, because of the considerable lie, both thumbs are at the front of the shaft, pointing down. Extensive tests have shown that this grip is the most effective one for putting.

Putting grip viewed from the side.

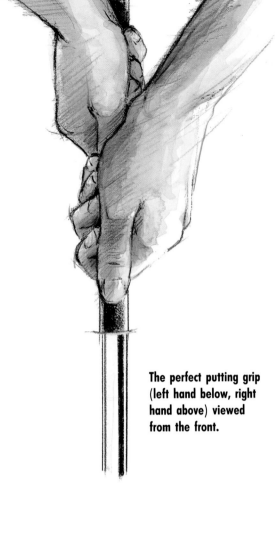

The perfect putting grip (left hand below, right hand above) viewed from the front.

This grip has three essential advantages:

1. The position of the right hand prevents flexion of the left hand, as is the case with the conventional grip (right hand below the left).
2. The club moves almost in a straight path and has less chance to rotate.
3. If the ball is in an imaginary straight line extending from the left eye, it is much easier for the player to imagine and execute the pendulumlike movement since the left hand together with the shaft of the putter creates something like a pendulum.

Try this grip and, after a relatively short period of practice time, your success rate on the course will markedly increase.

To find out if your eyes line up with the intended line to the target, drop a ball at a point that is directly below your left eye. Your body should be parallel to the intended line, and your hands should line up vertically below your right shoulder.

Viewed from the side, the putter moves on a straight line, back and forth, without being rotated. Your shoulders do not rotate but dip forward, swaying like a hanger on a clothes rack.

Position the putter so that you are close to the ball, and your eyes are vertical to the intended line to the target. This makes aiming much easier. In contrast to long drives, your head only moves in one direction in order to see the target. Be sure that your left eye looks directly down on the ball, because the putter is at its deepest point here, preventing the putter from hitting the ball during the backswing or the downswing. To check if your posture is correct, drop a second ball in line with your left eye. If this ball hits the one on the ground, your left eye is in line with the intended line to the target.

To make aiming easier, make sure that your body is parallel to the intended line to the target. Try to imagine railroad tracks. The right rail represents the intended line to the target, where the ball moves into the hole, and the left rail is the line parallel to it on which the body orients itself (lower arms, shoulders, hips, feet).

Often a player lines up his body on the line leading directly to the target. This is wrong. If you do this, a straight putt will end up on the right side of the hole. If you line up correctly, an imaginary line con-

necting your feet is as far to the left of the hole as the distance between you and the ball.

In previous discussions, we have assumed that the putt moves in a straight line without a break. In reality, that is seldom the case on the course. Imagine that the intended line to the target is the continuation of the direction the ball assumes at the start.

As we have already mentioned, it is very important that your hands (when viewed from the side) line up correctly below your shoulders. When you allow both arms to hang vertically from your shoulders, you know that the putter will swing back and forth without any danger of rotating.

Some additional points you will no doubt recognize when looking at the photos: In the putting position, the whole base of the club must touch the ground since, otherwise, the loft (approximately four degrees) will cause the ball to start out to the left if the tip of the clubhead is in the air or to the right when the heel of the clubhead is in the air.

Line your feet up vertically to the intended line to the target. In contrast to

long drives, where your feet turn slightly to the outside, here the lower part of your body remains motionless.

One more word about the position of the ball: In order to understand how the position of the ball influences the success of your shot, you must know what happens after the moment of impact. In the beginning, the ball doesn't roll; rather, it glides over the ground, because at the moment of impact, it only receives momentum towards the target. The friction of the grass against the underside of the ball breaks the gliding phase and, from that point on, the ball begins to roll. As soon as the speed of the forward movement equals that of the rolling movement, the ball stops its glide and rolls until it comes to a stop.

Since hitting the ball with the club in either the backswing or the downswing has little impact on the gliding phase of the ball, and, consequently, executing a clean stroke is difficult, it is imperative that you place the ball at a point where the club is at the lowest point in its swing. This point must be precisely in line with the left eye.

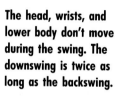

The head, wrists, and lower body don't move during the swing. The downswing is twice as long as the backswing.

Since, when putting, the ball should neither go up in the air nor roll a great distance, it is necessary for the body and the wrists to remain still during the swing. As a matter of fact, to achieve the greatest precision in putting, as few parts of the body as possible should be in motion. All that is necessary for the putter to move back and forth is for the shoulders to move like a pendulum. This means that they only move up and down and not (as in long drives) forward and backwards. Imagine that your shoulders are a clothes hanger swinging on a clothes rack. Your head and the lower part of your body take no part in the movement, so your weight doesn't shift.

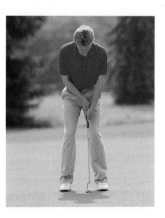

This shoulder movement assures that the hands and the head of the putter move exactly parallel to the intended line to the target. Making circular movements, where the putter head opens and closes, is not correct here. To avoid rotating the club-head and making it more difficult to gauge your stroke, keep your wrists absolutely passive.

To make it easier to get a feel for how much backswing advances a ball how far forward, hit the ball during the forward movement and don't attempt to break. The reason for this can be seen when watching a boccie game. A player will not pull his hand back immediately after releasing the ball; but rather, the arm will "follow through," and the length of this follow-through is always greater than the backswing. Expressed in a formula, the ratio between the backswing and follow-through is approximately 2:3.

In analyzing the play of top golfers, something very interesting became clear— the duration of a swing, measured from the start of the backswing to the moment of impact (regardless of the length of the putt) was about one second and was identical for each player. This means that for a short putt, both backswing and follow-through are relatively slow and that for long putts, the club moves considerably faster. To practise this particular aspect, the advanced player may use a metronome. However, beginners should first work on establishing the proper technique.

During the putt, the putter moves on a straight path without rotation. The ratio between the backswing and the follow-through is about 2:3.

As your putting technique improves, it is imperative that you learn how to read the green. Pros always take a long time doing it. Acquiring this skill should be a part of your practice routine.

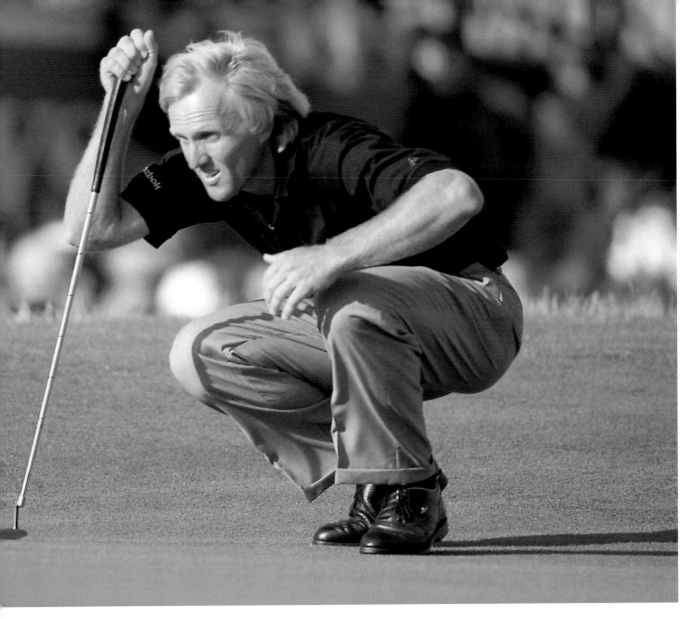

Putt Training

Empirical studies have proven that normal practice (putting several balls from one hole to another on the putting green) is effective for those players who do not have a feel for gauging their strokes. More advanced players, however, will not notice a marked improvement in their game.

For that reason, it's best to organize your training as follows:

- Fifty percent of the time should be set aside for practising the three different aspects that influence the moment of impact. Players who are just beginning to learn this system should dedicate the first five hours to these exercises.

- Thirty percent should be set aside for practising the security zone game (discussed later).
- Twenty percent of the time should be dedicated to practising long putts.

During our discussion about the success rate in putting, we determined that a great number of balls do not reach the hole because of the condition of the ground surrounding it. For the ball to overcome the elevated terrain immediately surrounding the hole without changing direction, the ball has to move at a certain speed. Balls that reach the hole on their very last rotation very rarely actually fall into the hole.

A ball moves at the proper speed when (assuming that it misses the hole) it rolls no more than 18 inches (45 cm) past the hole (see also page 103). This is very important because a ball that moves more slowly has a reduced putting success rate.

This factor is taken into consideration in the security-zone game. In this game, the player chooses a hole 3 to 18 feet (1–5 m) away from him and tries to hole the ball. The player is allowed five strokes for each hole, with the exception of the last hole (here the number of strokes is unlimited). If the ball is not farther behind the hole than the length of one putter, the player can putt the ball where it is. If the ball stops in front of the hole, is farther behind the hole than the length of one putter, or is to the side of it, the ball is not in the security zone. In this case, the player moves the ball one additional putter length away from the hole. As a matter of course, after every third stroke, move the ball the length of one putter farther from where it came to a stop. More advanced players can play a double security zone game. Here you always put the ball the length of one putter away from where it came to a stop if it has reached the security zone, and always two lengths away when it misses the security zone or when you don't hole the ball with two tries.

The following game is designed to practise long putts: Putt three balls each at a distance of 30, 45, and 60 feet (10, 14, and 18 m), trying to bring the balls to a stop within 3, 5, and 6 feet (1, 1.4, and 1.8 m).

Playing the security zone game is lots of fun, providing you have reached a certain level of skill. Compared with counting strokes on the putting green, the game quickly separates the good and the poor players.

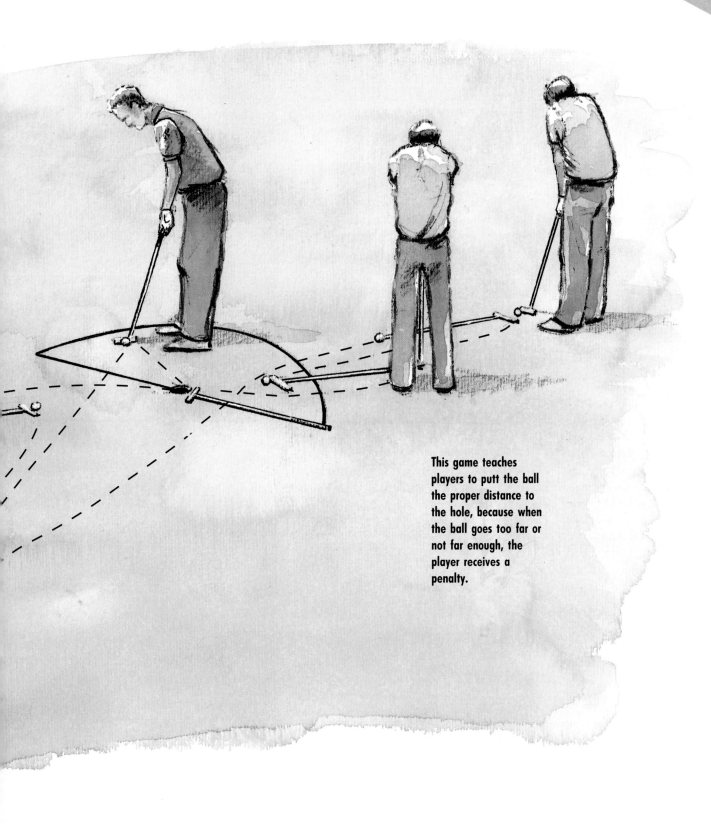

This game teaches players to putt the ball the proper distance to the hole, because when the ball goes too far or not far enough, the player receives a penalty.

Repeat this sequence until you have made a total of 27 putts. The game is finished as soon as you have made three more putts from 60 feet (18 m) away that come to a stop within 6 feet (1.8 m). If you have not made the 30 putts, continue practising for a total of 15 minutes.

Putting only one hole alone is not helpful because you don't practise "reading" the green. It is truly interesting how few golfers practise this on the putting green. Sad to say, there is no trick that will help you avoid having problems recognizing the right path. It is simply a matter of experience, requiring consistent practice. Players who don't practise this skill should not be surprised by their lack of success.

Here's a little trick to avoid the cone-shaped area around a hole on the putting green where holes are changed less often and the immediate areas around them are relatively high. Find a spot that hasn't had too much traffic and put four tees in the ground, making your own hole, so to speak. Now try to hit the balls through the tees. You can also add another tee 18 inches (45 cm) farther away, allowing you to determine if a "holed" ball was moving at the ideal speed.

Make your own hole on the putting green, using four tees placed in the ground.

I hope that I have been able to convince you that effective putting is not an inborn talent. Don't give up when, even after intensive practice sessions, you play a round without a successful putt. Remember that, in spite of having read the green perfectly and having executed your stroke perfectly, the ball can still roll past the hole. If you are patient and use the correct techniques, your success rate will increase over time.

When choosing a putter, make sure that the bulk of the weight is in the heel and the tip . . .

PUTTING

- No reliable feedback is available from putting. A ball can miss the hole by a wide margin because it is not perfectly round, the grass surface is uneven, there are footprints in the grass, there is an elevated area surrounding the hole, etc. In addition, you cannot ascertain the situation at impact from the way the ball moves, because different mistakes can have the same result.

- To gain reliable feedback, you have to practise the three different factors that influence the action at impact: the path of the putter, the positioning of the clubface at the moment of impact, and the club hitting the ball with the sweet spot.

- With the proper grip, your left hand is below your right hand.

- The proper position requires that your body be parallel to the intended line to the target, that your left eye be above the ball, and that your arms extend straight down from the shoulders.

- During the swing, your shoulders move like a pendulum above the intended line to the target. Your head and legs remain totally motionless. The speed of the club increases as it moves through the ball.

. . . and that the club is well balanced. The clubface should be parallel to the ground when you balance the putter on one finger.

Chipping

A chip is a flat approach shot used for distances between 11 and 65 yards (10–60 m) when there are no obstacles between the ball and the flag. The flight path is flat, and the ball should roll a considerable distance after hitting the ground. The techniques for chipping are simpler than for pitching, a high approach shot. In addition, a chip shot is more reliable because from the start you anticipate that the ball will move on a flat curve. In case the attempt misfires (topping), the distance that the ball covers might still be right. On the other hand, when you top a pitch, the ball usually goes way beyond the target because you are assuming from the start that the flight path will be high.

However, don't chip if you intend to reach the fairway. For instance, if the flag is very close to the near side of the green, the ball won't roll beyond the flag. In

Hold the 9 iron a little more at an angle than is required for the lie. On this plane, the club swings back and down through the ball. During the backswing, the path of the club seems steeper and more closed (rotated to the left) when compared to a full swing.

other words, you cannot categorically state that you use the chip shot for a short approach and the pitch for a long approach. The decision depends on the prevailing situation. If the flag is far away, in the back of a 100-foot (30-m) green, and the ball is about 65 feet (20 m) in front of it, a 165-foot (50-m) chip shot would be the right choice. However, if you have a choice between a chip or a pitch, always choose the chip.

The two basic chips are the standard chip and the putt chip. For a short distance, use the putt chip; for a longer distance—from 50 feet (15 m) on—use the standard chip.

Use the normal grip for chipping. However, move your hands down slightly. Place the ball a little to the right of center. The main movement involves the arms and shoulders. The body and the wrists remain passive.

Standard Chip

In contrast to the pitch (in which you use a sand wedge), when chipping, the ball should remain on a flat flight path. For this, you need a club with a slightly inclined face. The recommended club is usually a 7 iron. However, this club is somewhat long and has a very flat lie, requiring the player to stand rather far away from the ball. The 9 iron does not have these disadvantages and can (with the proper approach position and with both hands in front of the ball) be turned into a 7 iron.

I consider it a problem when a player constantly changes his club, attempting to adjust to different distances and situations. Except for extremely long chips, where you can use the 7 iron, stick with the 9 iron, since it represents the fastest

way of getting a sense for distances (the most important factor in chipping).

For a chip shot, use your normal grip, but allow your hands to slide down on the handle somewhat. The club will become even more handy for short shots.

Since body movement plays less of a role when chipping, and since precision and not distance is the deciding factor, posture and stance differ from longer drives as follows:

- In order to keep the distance to the ball as short as possible (increasing precision and making aiming easier), set the club on the ground somewhat more upright than the lie requires. This puts the heel of the club slightly in the air.
- Stand closer to the ball since the lack of body movement does not require additional support.

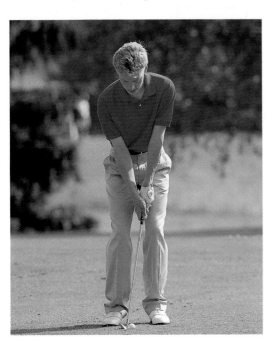

- Place the left foot slightly back so that the left leg does not interfere with the follow-through, but the body should still remain parallel to the intended line to the target.
- Place the hands (when viewed from the target) in front of the ball, which is to the right of center by the width of a ball. The whole upper body moves with the hands slightly to the left, shifting about 70 percent of the player's weight to the left foot.

To keep your wrists passive, particularly during the backswing, extend the length of the club with a second club. Use your wrists so that the clubhead is in front of your hands at impact. The shaft of the second club will hit you in the side.

During the back portion of the swing, the arms and shoulders dominate, while the wrists (except when hitting long chips) remain passive, and the weight is on the left foot. As is the case with long drives, the club moves back on exactly the same plane. Since this path of the swing is steeper, the clubface appears to be somewhat more closed, and the shoulders don't rotate but dip forward. This movement is similar to putting.

As with long drives, the club must be in a downward motion at impact. Of course, this is less prominent in the standard chip because the wrists are hardly involved during this downward motion, and the shot does not create a divot. Under no circumstances should you try to lift the ball in the air with a spooning motion. When chipping correctly, the club will hit the ball first and then brush the grass. Accomplishing this by bringing the hands back in front of the ball, exactly where they were at the approach. When viewed from the front, the club and the left arm must represent a straight line.

As is the case with all short strokes, the club should hit the ball as the speed is accelerating, making it easier to gauge your shot. This is accomplished by making the follow-through longer than the backswing. Since this technique is a rather simple one, after mastering the basics, you should constantly vary the target so that you can quickly acquire a sense for gauging this shot.

Putt Chip

The reverse overlap grip makes it possible for the 8 iron, used for the putt chip, to be held just as a putter.

If a target is less than 50 feet (15 m) away, choose the putt chip. It is a combination of the standard chip with movements similar to those of the putt. When using the standard chip, the wrists automatically flex to a small extent, and the club usually develops too much speed for a short distance. When using the putt-chip method, the wrists remain absolutely still.

Use this method when the distance to the hole is such that you could also putt the ball; for example, where too much high grass stands between the ball and the green to guarantee a successful shot. The 8 iron is the ideal club because the flight path of the ball should be lower than with the standard chip. When making the putt chip, set the 8 iron on the ground just like the putter, meaning that the angle at which the club moves past the hands is not quite as steep. Here, we use the reverse overlap grip, a grip that is often used for putting. The handle of the club lies between the hand and the thumb pads of the left hand. The back of the left hand points straight in the direction of the target. The left thumb rests precisely on the front side of the handle. At the outset, the left index finger remains free and crosses the fingers of the right hand only after the right hand is in position. The pad of the little finger of the right hand comes to rest on the last three fingers of the left hand. The right thumb is also on the handle and points in the direction of the clubhead.

The back of the right hand points straight in the direction of the target. Place the index finger of the left hand across the finger of the right hand, almost parallel to the shaft, preventing the left wrist from any dorsal flexion during the forward movement.

The posture and stance are the same for the putt chip as for putting. Line up your eyes over the intended line to the target.

For the putt chip, play the ball exactly at the midpoint between your feet with your hands slightly in front of the ball. The movement is identical to that used for putting. Set the club in motion using only a side-to-side rocking motion of the shoulders. Your wrists and body remain totally passive.

Place the ball in the middle of the stance so that the hands are slightly in front of it and the body is parallel to the intended line to the target.

The swing is identical to that used for putting. The shoulders don't rotate; they tilt side-to-side. Make sure that the club remains lined up with the intended line to the target without rotating. The body and wrists remain absolutely passive. For simplicity's sake, the club should increase in speed as it hits through the ball.

Hold the club in the same vertical position as the putter and move it back and forth on a straight line without rotation.

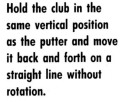

CHIPPING

- The hands are lower when chipping, and the club (9 iron) is positioned more vertical on the ground.
- The ball is a little to the right of center of the narrow, slightly open stance, so that the hands are in front of the ball.
- Arm and shoulder movements dominate during the backswing, while the body and wrists remain absolutely passive.
- The club moves down and through the ball so that, after impact, the clubhead brushes over the grass.
- The follow-through is somewhat longer than the backswing, so that the club hits the ball in the acceleration phase.
- For the putt chip, the player uses the reverse overlap grip.
- The posture, stance, and swing for the putt chip are identical to those used for putting, except that the ball is squarely in the center of the stance.

Pitching

The pitch is a high approach shot used when the distance to the flag is between 10 and 90 yards (10–80 m). The ball flies high in the air and, because of backspin, comes to a stop as quickly as possible after hitting the ground. Golfers distinguish between the standard pitch, 30 to 90 yards (25–80 m), and the short pitch, 10 to 30 yards (10–25 m).

The pitch differs from a drive in the length of the backswing, which depends on the distance the ball needs to travel, and the fact that during the rotation in the forward swing, the lower body does not move too far ahead of the upper body, as is the case during long drives.

Standard Pitch

The standard pitch is not a special shot like the chip, but simply a smaller version of the full swing.

The sand wedge (or any special wedge with more than 56 degree loft) is the club of choice for the standard pitch. Many players hesitate to use this club if they aren't in a bunker. However, the placement of the hands, in front of the ball, neutralizes the bounce. The sand wedge has an advantage over the pitching wedge because the former has more loft, giving the ball more height during flight and

more backspin after the ball hits the ground. Use the pitching wedge only when you cannot reach the green with the sand wedge.

This is not a special shot because the technique is almost identical to that used for long drives. The main difference is in the backswing. Depending on the distance, it is shorter for short distances and longer for longer distances. The grip and posture are the same as those for long drives. The stance can be slightly more open so that the lower body, because of the shorter swing, is already out of the way, which means that the left foot is slightly back. The shoulders should remain lined up with the intended line to the target. The player divides his weight equally between his feet. The ball is in the center of the stance, and the hands (when viewed from the target) are slightly in front of it.

Because the swing is short, the movement of the body is not that important. The main emphasis is on the movement of the arms and hands. The player must make sure that the hands flex properly during the backswing and that the end of the club is always pointing in the direction of the target. Since you have less time to compensate if your club is not moving in the proper plane, you can have problems here, particularly when the club moves too far to the inside, and you hit the ball too hard from there. This usually leads to a fat hit in which you push or hit the ball with the socket.

During the pitch, one end of the club must always point in the direction of the target because there is no time for adjustment.

Compared to a drive, the speed of the clubhead is not very fast and the vertical angle at impact is steeper. Consequently, the lower body will be ahead of the upper body in its rotation—the opposite of what happens during a long drive.

When pitching, the club must strike the ball on the downward movement. This means that the club hits the ball before it hits a divot. When hit full-force with a wedge, the divot from a pitch is deeper than with any other shot because of the extremely vertical club plane and the lower ball. You can only hit down if, at impact, your hands (viewed from the front) are in front of the ball and the club is hit through the ball inside-to-in. Many players try to spoon the ball. Probably subconsciously, they are trying to lift the ball into the air. However, you must avoid spooning the ball because this often leads to topping the ball or to fat hits, especially when the lie is bad. The angle of the face of the sand wedge is sufficient to drive the ball high in the air. The angle also assures you that the ball will stop quickly because of the backspin.

When pitching, hit the ball with a downward movement. Drive through the ball at the proper plane. At impact, your hands should be in front of the ball.

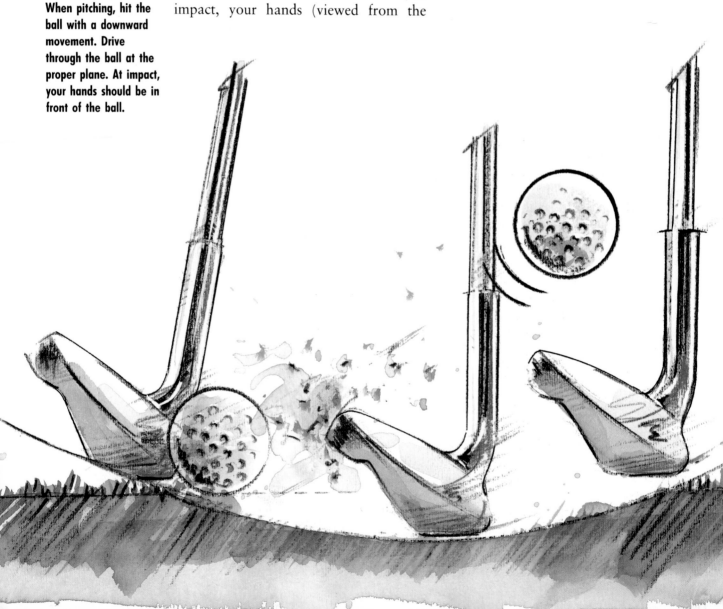

Short Pitch

You use the short pitch when the distance to the target is between 10 and 30 yards (10–25 m), and, even though the distance suggests a chip shot, the ball has to come to a quick stop. For the short pitch, you need to use a different technique because, when using the standard pitch, the ball goes too far due to the action of the wrists. The movement for the short pitch is similar to that of the chip. The difference is mainly in the choice of the club and the position of the ball. The 9 iron used for chipping does not hit the ball high enough in the air. For that reason, you use a sand wedge. The ball should be in the center of the stance and not, as is necessary for chipping, to the right of center. These two changes make the ball fly higher, as if chipped. Just as in chipping, the wrists remain passive. Here, too, the club moves through the ball on the downward motion, brushing the grass after impact.

PITCH

- The sand wedge is the ideal club for the pitch.
- The stance must be slightly open, but the shoulders must remain parallel to the intended line to the target.
- The lower body is not quite as far ahead of the upper body as for long drives, causing the club to hit the ball on a steeper angle.
- The grip, stance, posture, and swing are the same as for a full swing except for the length of the downswing and the two points made above.
- The short pitch is similar to the chip in that the ball is in the center of the stance.

Bunker Shot

Many golfers fear the bunker shot. Actually, it is a much easier shot than you might think because the swing is identical to that of the pitch. In addition, the club never hits the ball; you only hit the sand below the ball. It is the sand that pushes the ball. In contrast to other approach shots, you don't hit the ball and then the ground. A regular shot, in which the ball starts out on a low curve before gaining height, would not be useful. In order to clear the edge of the bunker, the ball has to get into the air immediately. In addition, there is little room for downswing errors in the bunker because the club slows down considerably if it hits the sand too early. In contrast, the club usually slices through the ball and loses very little speed on grass.

When a player assumes that the club will hit the sand before the ball, gauging the shot becomes much easier. The ball flies into the air immediately, clears even high bunker edges, and stops quickly after hitting the ground.

Players often avoid this shot by trying to chip or putt out of the bunker. This might work in isolated, individual cases. But most of the time, it doesn't succeed, and you still need an explosion shot. This is a bunker shot used for distances of up to 55 yards (50 m) in which the sand is thrown into the air as if from an explosion.

Of course, a player confronts numerous situations in bunkers. I will only address three of them: the standard bunker shot from a green bunker up to 33 yards (30 m), the long explosion shot from a bunker up to 55 yards (50 m) from the flag, and the shot required when the ball has been driven into the ground.

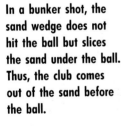

In a bunker shot, the sand wedge does not hit the ball but slices the sand under the ball. Thus, the club comes out of the sand before the ball.

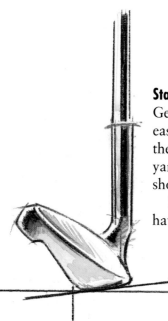

Standard Bunker Shots

Generally speaking, a ball in a bunker is easy enough to hit. If that is the case, and the distance to the flag is no more than 33 yards (30 m), use the standard bunker shot.

For a bunker shot to be successful, you have to use a sand wedge. This club has a sole specially designed for the explosion shot. When the shaft is at a right angle to the ground, the sole is not, as is the case with other clubs, parallel to the ground. Rather, it points in the air at a 7 to 11 degree angle. This means that the front edge is farther away from the ground than the back edge. When it strikes the ground, the clubhead won't dig too deeply into the ground. The principle behind it is similar to that of a flat stone which, when tossed at an angle into the water, won't sink, but jumps up in the air.

You must make three changes in your technique when using the standard pitch:

1. To avoid changing the swing, position the ball farther to the left than for the pitch. This allows the club to dig into the sand and hit a flat disk from below the ball.

The front edge of the sole of a sand wedge is above the lower edge, allowing the head to slide through the sand rather than digging into it.

The position of your body is slightly to the left of the intended line to the target, since the sand disk completely neutralizes the open clubface ...

For a bunker shot, the ball is opposite your left foot, allowing the club to hit the sand before the ball. The clubface rotates 20 degrees to the right before your hand grips the handle, so that the front edge of the sole of the club is even higher than normal, which permits the club ...

2. When hitting out of a bunker, the clubface rotates at least 20 degrees (tilted to the right), so that the head does not dig too deeply into the sand. The wedge face points to the right before your hands grip the handle, so that the relationship of your hands to your body is identical to that for long drives.

If the clubface tilted that way when driving from the fairway, the ball

would end up far to the right of the target. This is seldom the case in the bunker because the sand disk neutralizes any rotation. The club never makes contact with the ball, and the sand disk pushes ahead of the club. In addition, a sand wedge closes again rather easily because the heel of the clubhead slows down somewhat due to the fact that it is ahead of the tip. In other words, the golfer does not need to orient himself to the left of the intended line to the target because the club is to the right. Proper positioning depends on so many factors that, for all practical purposes, a player must experiment. In general, the player ought to position himself

... and because the clubhead closes when in the sand, and the position of the ball is to the left of the center of the stance.

between 5 and 10 degrees to the left of the target.

3. Given the same distance to the flag, the backswing for the bunker shot must be longer than for a shot played from the fairway since the club loses considerable speed when hitting the sand. A player must overcome the temptation to reduce the backswing when the target is only a short distance away, even if some of the balls go far beyond the target, usually the result of faulty technique. The swing is identical to that of the standard pitch. Do not try to manipulate the club when hitting under the ball. It will automatically hit the sand 2 inches (5 cm) in front of the ball (because of the position of the ball) and produce a divot 6 inches (15 cm) long and 1 inch (3 cm) wide. There will always be sand between the ball and the clubhead, with the sand pushing the ball forward and up. At impact, the club slows down considerably more with the bunker shot than with other shots because of the amount of sand pushed up in the air, making it necessary to pay special attention to the follow-through. The length of the backswing regulates the distance of the shot.

... to slide even more easily over the sand and lift the ball higher into the air. The follow-through for the bunker shot is also longer than the backswing.

- Place the ball opposite and in the middle of the left foot.
- Before gripping the handle, rotate the face of the sand wedge by 20 degrees.
- Given equal distances, the backswing for a bunker shot is longer than for a pitch.
- If a ball is deep in the sand, stand so that it is slightly to the right of the center of your stance. Close the face of the sand wedge slightly.
- The clubs of choice for long bunker shots, up to 55 yards (50 m), are the 9 and 7 irons, also used for standard bunker shots.

If the ball is deep in the sand, the clubface should be straight or slightly closed so that the clubhead can penetrate the sand sufficiently. However, the ball will probably start at a lower curve and roll farther than when hit with a normal bunker shot.

If bunker shots are still a problem, even after you have followed these techniques exactly and practised diligently, your pitching technique might be faulty. This is difficult to determine because a well-positioned ball on the grass is more forgiving than a ball in the bunker. If such is the case, go back and improve your pitching technique and then try the bunker shot again.

Trapped Ball

If a ball is deep in the sand, the club needs to hit a deeper sand disk in order to lift the ball in the air. Compared to a shot with a ball in good position, the clubhead should not hit the sand too early because it slows down too much.

To get ready for this shot, the ball is closer to the right foot, slightly to the right of the center of the stance. The position of the hands remains unchanged, so that they (viewed from the target) are in front of the ball. This assures a much steeper angle at impact, assuming that the hands are in the same position. It also lets the clubhead sink deeper into the sand.

The clubface is straight and may, if the ball is very deep in the sand, even be closed (rotated to the left). This will bring the front edge of the clubhead behind the lower edge, so that it can dig deeper into the sand. Because the clubface is in an upright position, it must be parallel to the intended line to the target.

Because of the large amount of sand involved, compared to the distance, the backswing must be even longer than if the ball were in a good situation.

Keep in mind that the ball, when compared to the standard bunker shot, will start out on a much flatter curve and roll farther after hitting the ground.

Long Explosion Shot

Use the long explosion shot when the distance to the flag is between 33 and 55 yards (30–50 m). The standard bunker shot is not suitable because, for an explosion shot with a sand wedge, the distance to the flag is too far. A standard pitch won't work—the club should not hit the ground in front of the ball because that would leave the ball way short.

You should make use of the fact that most bunkers have very low edges, so the ball can start out on a flat curve, which suggests a 9 to 7 iron. The hitting technique is identical to that of the standard bunker shot. However, because you are using a different club, the ball will fly lower and farther.

To get a feeling for distance and to learn which club to use, always practise this shot before using it on the course.

The position of the ball should be slightly to the right of the center of your stance. In this way, the clubhead does not hit the sand too far away from the ball.

The Kananakis Golf
Club at the edge of the
Rocky Mountains is
typical of Canadian golf
courses—lots of natural
water traps and
streams. Sometimes,
you even meet bears
and elks.

Appendices

Effective Warm-Ups

A sensible, effective warm-up is as important for the golfer as it is for any other athlete. It is too bad that golfers think they are the absolute exception. Although they would probably not allow their car to plunge into a race while the engine is still cold, when it comes to their own body, they have no problem going full tilt as soon as they are on the course.

The few who do warm-ups and stretching exercises usually do them poorly, using traditional exercises that are often quite harmful to their backs. These exercises might include: rotating the upper body, bending over, and stretching with a hollow back. Many players add exaggerated bounces to their stretches, causing tendons and ligaments to overextend.

A proper warm-up is not simply a means of preventing injuries such as strains and torn muscles. Exercises also increase mobility in the joints and improve overall coordination.

The warm-up should begin with movements involving the whole body to energize the cardiovascular system. Running in place, arm movements, and body and arm stretching are also effective.

These are followed by stretching exercises that add mobility. Make sure that you start out by stretching gently, adding more extensive stretches slowly and over time.

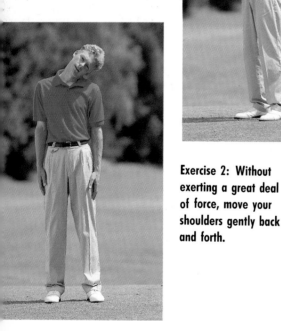

Exercise 1: In a continuous movement, bend your head to the left, right, and forward, but not to the rear.

Exercise 2: Without exerting a great deal of force, move your shoulders gently back and forth.

Exercise 3: Pull your left or right arm to the opposite side of your body.

Conclude your warm-up with golf-specific exercises, such as test swings. Use swings with a closed stance (feet next to each other), baseball swings (head of the club at hip level), and side-reversed swings (right-hander like left-hander and vice versa).

You will quickly realize that your first swings are much more successful when you do warm-ups and stretch your muscles. Take at least 10 to 15 minutes for the following program:

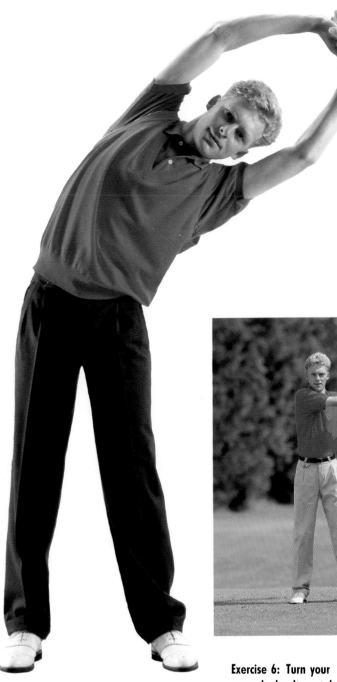

Exercise 4: Put one hand between your shoulder blades, reach over with your other hand, and hold the elbow of the arm, pulling the arm gently behind your head. Increase the pull slightly over time.

Exercise 5: Put your hands together and stretch both arms over your head. Flex your knees with your legs together and bend your upper body alternately to the left and to the right. No hollow backs!

Exercise 6: Turn your upper body alternately to the right and the left while turning your hips in the opposite direction.

Exercise 8: While standing, grab the ankle of your right or left foot and pull the foot up to your seat. Both thighs should remain parallel to each other, and the leg you stand on should be straight. No hollow backs!

Exercise 7: Alternate between lifting your heels and your toes off the floor.

Exercise 9: Lean your straight upper body over the thigh of your bent leg, allowing the other leg to get a good stretch. Alternate legs.

Exercise 10: Lean sideways and point the toes of your bent leg slightly to the outside. During the alternating stretch, both feet are solidly on the ground. Without force, slowly increase the bend of the knees. Keep your back straight throughout.

Glossary

Address position: The position of the golfer after having assumed his stance and positioned his club.

Angle at impact: The angle of the clubhead between the intended line to the target and the horizontal component of the path of the club just prior to impact. It can only be seen from the side. Ideally, the club hits through the ball inside-to-in. The force depends on the club: short club, less force; long club, more force. Possible deviations are:

1. The path of the curve moves outside-to-in.
2. The path of the curve moves inside-to-out (the horizontal angle at impact).

The angle between the ground and the vertical component of the path of the club immediately before impact can only be viewed from the front. Ideally, when using an iron, the club swings through the ball from above and down. When using a wood that is parallel to the ground and when teeing off with a wood, the club swings from below and up. This is the vertical angle at impact.

Approach shot: A short shot to the green using a reduced swing.

Backspin: The rotation of the ball around its own axis against the direction of the flight. (Every ball in flight has a backspin, otherwise it would fall back to the ground immediately.) Backspin is not just a factor after the ball hits the ground, but if the ball rolls back, it has a particularly strong backspin. The loft of the clubhead creates backspin.

Bulge: The horizontally rounded clubface of a wood.

Chip: A flat approach shot.

Dipping: A rotation of the shoulders towards a steep plane. (The left shoulder is too low; the right shoulder is too high.)

Divot: A piece of grass cut out with a club.

Dorsal flexion: Bending the wrist in the direction of the back of the hand.

Downswing: The part of the swing starting at the end of the backswing to the moment of impact.

Draw: A shot that curves slightly to the left.

Explosion shot: A bunker shot in which the player deliberately hits the sand before hitting the ball. The club hits a slice of sand underneath the ball, allowing the ball to fly out of the bunker. The sand flies out of the bunker like an explosion.

Fade: A shot that curves slightly to the right.

Fat hit: A shot in which the clubhead hits the ground in front of the ball. This shortens the length of the flight considerably.

Follow-through: The part of the swing from the moment of impact to the forward end position.

Hook: A shot that starts out in the direction of the target and then veers to the left.

Iron Byron: A robot that simulates a golf swing, named after Byron Nelson, the golf

pro. Almost all manufacturers of clubs and golf balls have such a robot.

Leading edge: The lower front edge of the clubhead.

Lie of the club: The angle between the shaft of the club and the sole of the clubhead.

Loft: The angle of the clubface and a vertical line to the ground which lifts the ball into the air.

Pitch: A high approach shot.

Plane: A golf swing has numerous planes:

1. The club plane is defined by the lie of the club.
2. The arm plane is the angle of the left arm (when viewed from the side).
3. The shoulder plane is the angle created by the left and right upper sides of the shoulder during a swing (viewed from the side).

A plane is flat when oriented horizontally and steep when oriented vertically.

Point of release: The moment during the downswing when the angle between the left lower arm and the club begins to increase.

Pre-shot routine: A routine the player uses before starting the swing. Ideally, it is always the same.

Pronation: The rotation of the lower arm in the direction of the side of the thumb.

Pull: A ball that starts to the left and then flies straight.

Push: A ball that starts out to the right and then flies straight.

Radial flexion: Flexing the wrists in the direction of the thumb.

Reverse pivot: A faulty body movement during the swing in which the player shifts his weight to the wrong side during the backswing and downswing, respectively.

Shank: A ball hit with the socket, or hose, of the club, causing the ball to veer to the right or left.

Skinny shot: A shot is skinny if the club strikes the ball too high but still below the equator of the ball. The flight curve of the ball is flat, and the ball has less backspin

Slice: A ball that starts out in the direction of the target and then veers off to the right.

Sole: The bottom of the clubhead.

Supination: The rotation of the lower arm in the direction of the little finger.

Trailing edge: The lower, back edge of the clubhead.

Ulnar flexion: Flexing the wrists in the direction of the little finger.

Upper end point: The highest point of the backswing.

Volar flexion: Flexing the wrists towards the palm of the hand.

Index

Photo Credits
Front cover: Bavaria Stock Imagery, Gauting
Back cover: Atelier G & M Köhler, Leonberg
Bongarts Sportfotografie GmbH, Hamburg: pp. 2–3; Henning Bangen: p. 12; Hardt Sportfoto, Int., Hamburg: pp. 4–5, 8, 10–11, 62, 112–113, 129; Gisela Kelbert, Idstein: pp. 83 above right, 108 above and below; William Diesbrook, Neustadt: pp. 1, 4–5, 6–7, 14–15, 19, 40–41, 50–51, 64–65, 70–71, 92–93, 94–95, 96–97, 134–135; Atelier G & M Köhler, Leonberg: all others

Thanks also go to Golf House Direct Company GmbH, Waterloohain 5, 22769 Hamburg, for making available the golf equipment for the photos in this book.

Drawings by Kurt Dittrich, Wiesbaden
Drawings adapted from *Putt Like the Pros* (1989) by Dave Pelz with Nick Mastroni: pp. 99, 100, 101, 102, 103, 104; and from *The Search for the Perfect Swing* (1968) by A. Cochran and J. Stobbs: p. 98

Edited by Claire Bazinet
Translated by Elisabeth Reinersmann

Library of Congress Cataloging-in-Publication Data

Heuler, Oliver.
   [Golf. English]
   Perfecting your golf swing : new ways to lower your score / by
Oliver Heuler ; [translated by Elisabeth Reinersmann].
      p. cm.
   Includes index.
   ISBN 0-8069-0875-0
   1. Swing (Golf) I. Title.
GV979.S9H48 1995
796.352′3—dc20
                                  95-20236
                                  CIP

10 9 8 7 6 5 4 3

Published 1995 by Sterling Publishing Company, Inc.
387 Park Avenue South, New York, N.Y. 10016
Originally published by FALKEN-VERLAG GmbH
under the title *Golf: Neue Wege zum erfolgreichen Spiel*
© 1993 by FALKEN-VERLAG GmbH Niedernhausen/Ts.
English translation © 1995 by Sterling Publishing Co., Inc.
Distributed in Canada by Sterling Publishing
% Canadian Manda Group, One Atlantic Avenue, Suite 105
Toronto, Ontario, Canada M6K 3E7
Distributed in Great Britain and Europe by Cassell PLC
Wellington House, 125 Strand, London WC2R 0BB, England
Distributed in Australia by Capricorn Link (Australia) Pty Ltd.
P.O. Box 6651, Baulkham Hills, Business Centre, NSW 2153, Australia
Printed and bound in Hong Kong
All rights reserved

Sterling ISBN 0-8069-0875-0